International Business Communication Standards

IBCS® Version 1.2

INTERNATIONAL BUSINESS COMMUNICATION STANDARDS

IBCS® VERSION 1.2

CONCEPTUAL, PERCEPTUAL, AND SEMANTIC DESIGN OF COMPREHENSIBLE BUSINESS REPORTS, PRESENTATIONS, AND DASHBOARDS

COMPILED AND EDITED BY ROLF HICHERT, JÜRGEN FAISST, AND MORE CONTRIBUTORS OF THE IBCS ASSOCIATION

ISBN 978-3-9821414-2-8

Published by IBCS Media, Hilden (Germany) 2022.

INTRODUCTION TO IBCS®

The International Business Communication Standards (IBCS) are practical proposals for the design of business communication. One focal point concerns the application of a semantic notation supporting the proper conceptual and perceptual design of charts and tables in reports, presentations, and dashboards.

THE SUCCESS FORMULA OF THE IBCS STANDARDS

Business Communication meets the *IBCS Standards* if it complies with the rules of the seven areas that form the acronym "SUCCESS" (the SUCCESS formula):

S AY **Convey a message**: Every real report should convey a message, otherwise it's just a data collection. To do so requires an introduction to the theme as well as credible evidence supporting the message.

U NIFY **Apply semantic notation**: Things that mean the same should look the same. This rule applies to all content, be it terminology, measurements, analyses, highlighting, etc.

C ONDENSE **Increase information density**: All information necessary to understanding the content should, if possible, be included on one page. Doing so requires good utilization of space and small yet easily recognizable objects and elements.

C HECK **Ensure visual integrity**: Information should be presented in the most truthful and the most easily understood way possible, avoiding improper scaling, manipulated representations and misleading visuals.

E XPRESS **Choose proper visualization**: The objects (e.g. diagrams, tables, pictures) selected should convey the desired message along with the underlying facts as intuitively as possible.

S IMPLIFY **Avoid clutter**: All components and characteristics, which are too complicated, redundant, distracting or merely decorative, should be avoided.

S TRUCTURE **Organize content**: Content should follow a logical structure. Corresponding elements should be consistent and exhaustive without any overlap.

CONCEPTUAL RULES

The *conceptual rules* from the SAY (convey a message) and STRUCTURE (organize content) sections of the SUCCESS formula help to clearly relay content by using an appropriate storyline. They are based on the work of authors such as Barbara Minto[1].

The conceptual rules were invented decades ago and have been the subject of training courses ever since. Their wide acceptance is based on scientific, experimental, and practical experience.

PERCEPTUAL RULES

The *perceptual rules* from the EXPRESS (choose proper visualization), SIMPLIFY (avoid clutter), CONDENSE (increase information density), and CHECK (ensure visual integrity) sections help to clearly relay content by using an appropriate visual design. They are based on the work of authors such as William Playfair[2], Willard Cope Brinton[3], Gene Zelazny[4], Edward Tufte[5] and Stephen Few[6].

The perceptual rules were invented decades ago and have been the subject of training courses ever since. Their wide acceptance is based on scientific, experimental, and practical experience.

SEMANTIC RULES

Yet many reports, presentations, and dashboards are still hard to understand or even violate the conceptual and perceptual rules. This is why the *semantic notation rules* of the UNIFY section have been invented by Rolf Hichert[7] and other contributors of the *IBCS Association*. Experiences from other disciplines and first studies in reporting[8] proof that a uniform notation *(IBCS Notation)* will not only help to clearly relay content by pattern recognition, but will also help to comply with the conceptual and perceptual rules of the SUCCESS formula.

---

[1] Minto, Barbara: The Pyramid Principle, 3rd edition, 2002
[2] Playfair, William: The Commercial and Political Atlas, 1786
[3] Brinton, Willard Cope: Graphic Methods For Presenting Facts, 1914
[4] Zelazny, Gene: Say it with charts, 4th edition, 2001
[5] Tufte, Edward: The Visual Display of Quantitative Information, 2nd edition, 2011
[6] Few, Stephen: Show Me the Numbers, 2nd edition, 2012
[7] Hichert, Rolf and Faisst, Jürgen: Solid, outlined, hatched – How visual consistency helps better understand reports, presentations and dashboards, 2019
[8] Freyer, Johannes et al: More than just a Standard - How IBCS facilitates the perception of business data: An eye-tracking and laboratory study at the Technische Universität München (TUM), 2019

The manifestation of semantic notation rules is a matter of convention rather than science. This is why the notation rules are suggested by the not-for-profit *IBCS Association* in a community-driven Creative Commons project. Wide acceptance will make them the de facto standard needed to recognize visual patterns in reports.

The UNIFY section of the SUCCESS formula constitutes a kind of umbrella over all other areas and sets IBCS apart from all existing report design principles. So this documentation starts with the introduction of semantic notation rules. It is followed by the chapters dealing with conceptual and perceptual rules and the positive impact of semantic notation on their compliance.

IBCS ASSOCIATION

The IBCS Standards are published for public use under the *Creative Commons Attribution Share-Alike 4.0 International License* (CC BY-SA) on www.ibcs.com/standards.

The review and further development of the IBCS Standards is an ongoing process controlled by the IBCS Association. The *IBCS Association,* a not-for-profit organization that publishes the Standards for free, engages in extensive consultation and discussion prior to issuing new versions. This includes worldwide solicitation for public comment.

FURTHER DEFINITIONS

This document uses some technical terms we would like to define as follows:

BUSINESS COMMUNICATION

For our purposes, *business communication* means sharing business information for analytical and reporting objectives. In this sense, we organize business communication into *products* (e.g. reports, presentations, statistics, analytic applications), consisting of one or more *pages* (e.g. PowerPoint slides, screens) comprised of *objects* (e.g. charts, tables, text, pictures) with both *specific elements* (e.g. columns, axes, labels) and *general elements* (e.g. titles, comments).

COMMUNICATION PRODUCTS

Communication products are compilations of information displayed on one or multiple (screen) pages such as reports, presentations, statistics, and interactive analytic applications. Colloquially, all communication products are also referred to as *reports* in the broader sense.

In a stricter sense, the term *report* was originally used to distinguish *written* documents with a predetermined structure from formal *verbal* communication products called *presentations*. For presentations, the visual design proposed by IBCS relates to the material used (*presentation material*) such as the slides projected during the presentation and the handouts distributed before or after. In this sense, the term *presentation* is also used as a short form for *presentation material*.

In the literal sense, the term *reports* is also used to distinguish communication products *reporting messages* from mere *data compilations* called *statistics*. In contrast to reports, the charts in statistics do not prove or explain a given message. They rather support finding a message, demanding active search and exploratory analysis by the user.

Whereas reports and statistics used to be printed and thus *static* in nature, today they are often subject to *interactive analytic applications*. These *management information systems* or *dashboards* are usually compilations of interactive *statistics* covering a certain business topic (e.g. analysis of sales). In rare cases they also enable the conveyance of editorially prepared messages, which makes them interactive *reports*, similar to an online newspaper.

Analytic applications are being built using information technology like analytic databases and Business Intelligence software.

The IBCS Standards can be used for the design of both *static* and *interactive* communication products.

COMMUNICATION PAGES

Single pages in a written report, one slide of a presentation or one screen view of an interactive analytic system are called *communication pages*. The page size and grid determines the layout.

The *size* of a page depends on the application and the media used to display the report. The IBCS Standards recommend a corporate-wide standardization of page sizes for the different communication products.

A thorough and consistent *grid* concept for the design of pages makes it easier to obtain an overview. The IBCS Standards recommend the development and use of corporate template grids for the most common page types and sizes as a part of a corporate report notation manual.

COMMUNICATION OBJECTS

The charts, tables, texts and pictures posted on a page are called *communication objects*. Communication objects represent an analytic view of a situation and can stand alone with or without a corresponding message.

COMMUNICATION ELEMENTS

Objects are comprised of *communication elements* such as object specific visualization elements (e.g. bars, columns, lines), legends, labels, axes, etc. In addition, *general elements* exist such as titles, footnotes, and messages, which are not used for the construction of objects but are necessary for the comprehension of objects and entire pages.

ACKNOWLEDGEMENTS

The IBCS Association would like to thank all contributors who helped transform the first drafts of IBCS into this version 1.2. With your comments on www.ibcs.com/standards and the subsequent discussions, you not only improved quality, but also became part of a community striving for further development of a generally accepted international standard.

CONTRIBUTORS (IN ALPHABETICAL ORDER)

Mohamed Abouyakob
Denis Abdulkerimov
Steve Adams
Todd Adler
Harry Anand
Juan Carlos Aranibar
Viola Arens
Thomas Bauer
Felix Becker
Erik Beekhuis
Nicole Bender
Mathias Besser
Dietrich Betz
Marcus Bitterlich
Raphael Branger
Peter Büschges
Gary Crawford
Paul Damen
Greg Davey
Slawomir Derkowski
Austin Diaz
Daniel Doorduin
Jörg Decker
Christian Ehm
Norbert Engelhardt
Jürgen Faisst
Holger Gerhards
Holger Gerths
Ralph Ginzinger
Michael Gill

Michael Gniffke
Bryan Gough
Kristof Gramm
Wolfgang Hackenberg
Tilman Hagen
Jens Herrmann
Rolf Hichert
Ronny Hoffmann
Beat Honegger
Jörn Johenneken
Stefan Kersten
Anna Knaub
Gunnar Knoch
Jörg Knuth
Piotr Kozak
Peter Kriebernegg
Tomasz Książyk
Michael Lai
Andrej Lapajne
Ronald van Lent
Severin Leuenberger
Timo Linde
Wilson Mar
Michael May
Daniel Meier
Claude-Henri Meledo
Shruthy Menon
Mladen Meter
Dietmar Meyersiek
Mark Michel

Imran Mohammed

Holger Morick

Petra Morschheuser

Mario Mühllechner

Ilya Mukovoz

Esin Özkan

Helge Paragenius

Tobias Piecha

Alexander Pröm

Manuel H. Ramírez

Grischa Rehmer

Markus Reith

Tobias Riedner

Kristian Rümmelin

Ilya Rykov

Antti Salmio

Bojan Šćepanović

Florian Schalowski

Michael Schelkle

Paul Schneider

Lars Schubert

Arne-Kristian Schulz

Michael Schwan

Ulrich Seidl

Jorge Sepulveda

Paresh Shah

Tilo Sommerwerk

Stefan Spittank

Christian Stein

Heinz Steiner

Jacqueline Strobel

Xavier Subirats

Edyta Szarska

Thomas Terbuch

Elias Teufel

Jevgeni Vitsenko

Nenad Vukovic

Markus Wolff

Jan Zeides

Volker Zeng

CONTENTS

STRUCTURE – ORGANIZE CONTENT 57

PERCEPTUAL RULES 67

EXPRESS: CHOOSE PROPER VISUALIZATION 68

SIMPLIFY: AVOID CLUTTER 113

CONDENSE: INCREASE INFORMATION DENSITY 120

CHECK: ENSURE VISUAL INTEGRITY 135

SEMANTIC RULES

Semantic rules help to clearly relay content by using a uniform notation *(IBCS Notation)*. The uniform notation suggested in the following UNIFY section of the SUCCESS formula will unleash the power of pattern recognition in visual perception. Semantic notation is thus a preparatory set of rules supporting the conceptual and perceptual report design principles that follow. The idea of a semantic report notation has been invented by Rolf Hichert. The rules are mainly based on the work of him and other contributors of the *IBCS Association*.

UNIFY – APPLY SEMANTIC NOTATION

UNIFY covers all aspects of applying semantic notation in reports, presentations, and dashboards.

Applying semantic notation means that reports follow this governing principle: *Similar content should be visualized in a similar manner;* what looks the same should also mean the same. On the flip side: If the content is not the same, it should not look the same.

In many specialized disciplines such as engineering, music, and architecture, *semantic notation standards* are a matter of course. The world of business communication lacks such notation standards, one of the main reasons management reports are sometimes hard to understand. For example, no common agreement on the meaning of various style elements such as titles, axes, highlighting indicators, etc. used in business charts exists yet.

This chapter covers semantic rules for all important and frequently recurring aspects of meaning in the context of business communication, such as terminology (e.g. words, abbreviations, number formats), descriptions (e.g. messages, titles, legends), dimensions (e.g. measures, scenarios, time periods), analyses (e.g. comparisons and variances), and indicators for highlighting, scaling and other purposes.

UN 1 UNIFY TERMINOLOGY

Terms are the non-visual part of business communication. Unified *terms and abbreviations* as well as unified formats for *numbers, units and dates* accelerate understanding.

UN 1.1 UNIFY TERMS AND ABBREVIATIONS

The standardization of terms and abbreviations in reports and presentations is achieved by using an unambiguous language and by unifying the usage of terms (glossary) within an organization.

Unify, compile and explain all terms and abbreviations in a clearly arranged corporate *glossary* including abbreviations and definitions, see Figure UN 1.1.

Term	Abbreviations short long		Definition
+Return on investment	ROI	Ret. on inv.	ROI is defined as...
+Accounts receivable	AR	Acc. receiv.	AR...
+Profit before tax	PBT	Profit b. tax	PBT...
+Profit and loss	P&L	Profit & loss	P&L...
+Human resources	HR	Human res.	HR...
+Net sales per capita	NS/c	NS per cap.	NS/c...

Figure UN 1.1: Unify terms and abbreviations

A glossary with terms and abbreviations in more than one language might be necessary in order to avoid different translations.

Often the names of business measures are too long for charts and tables. Use abbreviations instead. It might be a good solution to define *short abbreviations* (e.g. to *A/R* for *Accounts Receivable* be used in table *column* headers) and *long abbreviations* (e.g. *Acc. Receiv.* to be used in table *row* headers).

Unified terms and abbreviations for the notation of scenarios and time periods are covered in the respective sections.

UN 1.2 UNIFY NUMBERS, UNITS, AND DATES

Unify the formats for numbers, units and dates within an organization. This will enhance legibility, see Figure UN 1.2.

23 mtr.	100.000.000	23 m	100 000 000
34 kg.	123456	34 kg	123 456
20 sec.	1234567 CHF	20 s	1.23 mCHF
22 tons	€	22 t	EUR
[kg]	US$	kg	USD
sqm	£	m²	GBP
1.5.2021	II/2021	2021-05-01	2021-Q2
01/05/21	W17-2021	2021-05-01	2021-W17
05/01/21	Jun/2021	2021-05-01	2021-06

Figure UN 1.2: Unify numbers, units, and dates

Numbers

Different languages and countries use different *number formats*, e.g. 1.234.567,00 (DEU); 1,234,567.00 (USA); 1'234'567,00 or 1'234'567.00 (CHE).

It is important to unify the number formats in all communication products of an organization. A valid option is to use the notation as recommended by the *International System of Units (SI)* in "ISO 80000-1":

- Thousand delimiter: 1 234 (narrow blank space)
- Decimal sign: 1,23 or 1.23 (SI allows both versions)

Do not use long numbers in order to avoid distraction and to concentrate on the essentials, see also the SIMPLIFY rule SI 5.2 "Avoid long numbers". Use *currency prefixes* and *metric prefixes* to limit the number of digits to a maximum of three in charts and four in tables.

The most common formats for *negative values* are "-123" and "(123)". Use the same format for all negative values within an organization.

Positive values do not have a plus sign, unless they represent variances.

Currencies

Use consistent *currency abbreviations* across an organization such as the ones suggested by ISO 4217. ISO 4217 provides a set of currency abbreviations using three-letter acronyms such as EUR, CHF, USD, and GBP. The use of special currency symbols such as €, $, and £ is not recommended if a report includes many different currencies.

Use also consistent *metric prefixes* across an organization in combination with the currency units for monetary values expressed in thousands or millions. A good option is to use lower case characters to differentiate the prefixes from the currency abbreviations and use single digit metric prefixes to save space, such as "k" for thousand, "m" for million and "b" for billion. Below are examples of using single digit currency metric prefixes with EUR:

1 kEUR = 1 000 EUR

1 mEUR = 1 000 000 EUR

1 bEUR = 1 000 000 000 EUR

Physical units

For the consistent notation of *physical units* the International System of Units (SI) with units such as kg, t, m, km, etc. is a good choice.

In the case of non-monetary values expressed in thousands or millions, the *International System of Units* also suggests metric prefixes such as "G" for billion, "M" for million, and "k" for thousand.

Dates

A good choice for the consistent notation of *dates* is ISO 8601, an international standard covering the exchange of date and time-related data: YYYY-MM-DD, e.g. "2021-12-31".

Other significant notation principles regarding time-related aspects will be dealt in the UNIFY rule UN 3.3 "Unify time periods".

UN 2   UNIFY DESCRIPTIONS

Descriptions are textual elements that describe the visual elements in reports, presentations, and dashboards facilitating comprehension. The following suggests unified layouts for every kind of *descriptions*.

UN 2.1   UNIFY MESSAGES

The *message* the author intends to convey to the reader or audience (see also chapter SAY) is best recognized, if the position and the layout of the message is always the same, see Figure UN 2.1.

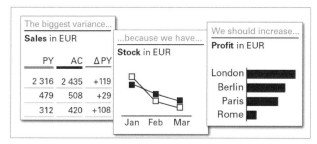

Figure UN 2.1: Unify messages

The *position* of messages should always be at the top of a report or presentation page, either a) above the title (see Figure UN 2.1-1) or b) right of the title. Position b) is not structured as clearly as position a) but it helps saving valuable vertical space especially on pages in landscape format. The exact position and notation of the message may vary from organization to organization but should be consistent across a single organization.

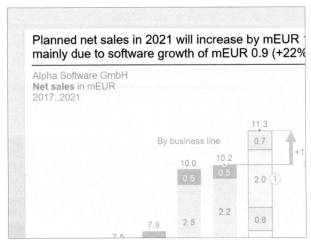

Figure UN 2.1-1: Message text lines (example)

The *wording*, *structuring* and *meaning* of messages is discussed in the IBCS part on "SAY".

UN 2.2 UNIFY TITLES AND SUBTITLES

Titles identify the content of pages and their objects in its entirety, without omitting anything that is needed to understand the content, see Figure UN 2.2. In contrast to messages, titles do not contain any evaluating aspects, such as interpretations, conclusions, or propositions.

Figure UN 2.2: Unify titles and subtitles

If there is more than one object on a page, use *page titles* for entire pages, slides, or screens and *subtitles* for different objects on a page. The combination of any title and applicable subtitle includes the name of the reporting unit, measure and time. Any elements that relate to the whole report page should be included in the page title, whereas any element which relates to a subset of the report should be included in the relevant subtitle.

PAGE TITLES

Page titles identify the content of a page. In general, it's a good choice to completely describe the content of a page with the following three lines:

Title line 1: Reporting unit ("who")

Element(s) of a structure dimension representing the object of the report, typically a legal entity, an organization unit, a line of business, a project, etc. or combinations thereof, e.g.

- ABC Corporation
- European division
- Project B
- ABC Corporation, European division, Project B

Add filter information if the elements are not exhaustive, e.g.

- International Chocolate Corporation, top ten clients
- International Chocolate Corporation, divisions with negative EBIT in 2021

If title line 1 becomes too long its content can be split into two lines, e.g.

- International Chocolate Corporation, European division
  Top ten clients

Title line 2: Business measure(s) ("what")

Element(s) of the measure dimension such as sales, profit, and shipment. Business measures are measured either in currency units (e.g. EUR, USD) or in physical units (e.g. #, kg, t). Use metric prefixes (e.g. k, m, b for monetary values) where appropriate. Measures are written in bold font, their units are written in regular font. Examples are:

- **Net sales** in mEUR
- **Net sales** in mEUR, **margin** in %
- **Headcount** in #

Use a suiting name for a *set of measures*, if more than two measures have to be presented on one page. Examples are:

- **Income statement** in kEUR
- **ROI tree** in mEUR
- **Balanced scorecard**
- **Product market portfolio**

Use footnotes if parts of the measures are redundant or if parts of the measures are of minor importance for understanding. Examples are:

- **Net sales** in mEUR (without intercompany sales) - simpler: **Net sales*** in mEUR

- **Operating margin** in mEUR (non-IFRS) - simpler: **Operating margin*** in mEUR

Additional information about the way presenting the content can help to understand better the respective page. They might concern structure dimensions, e.g.

- **Profit** in mUSD, by products
- **Net sales** in kEUR, by products and by countries

or they might be analytical annotations, e.g.

- **Net sales** in mEUR and **profit** in mEUR, sorted by net sales (↓)
- **Full time equivalents** in #, indexed (2018 = 100%)
- **Gross margin** in kUSD, top ten

or even combinations of structure dimensions and analytical annotations, e.g.

- **Net sales** in mEUR, by countries, sorted by net sales (↓)
- **Full time equivalents** in #, by offices, indexed (2018 = 100%)

If title line 2 becomes too long its content can be split into two lines, e.g.:

- **Full time equivalents** in #, by offices
  Indexed (2018 = 100%)
- **Net sales** in mEUR, by countries
  Sorted by net sales (↓)

Title line 3: Time period(s), scenario(s), and variance(s) ("when")

Element(s) of the time dimension (e.g. years, months), of the *scenario* dimension (e.g. actual, plan), and *variances* (e.g. ΔPL, ΔPL%) if necessary.

In general, elements of the *time* dimension (e.g. 2021, 2021-Q1) are necessary for understanding. Elements of the *scenario* dimension (e.g. AC, PL, FC) and *variances* are added if they help to understand the page content faster. If only actual values are presented, the attribute AC can be omitted.

Displaying the time element first works well if both time and scenario elements are shown in title line 3.

For better consistency you can use "&" (ampersand sign) when title elements together make up a time series, e.g. "AC&PL" (without blanks) if the first 8 months of a year present AC values and the last 4 months present PL values. Use "and" when different elements are presented for all time periods, e.g. "AC and PY" if all 12 months of a year present both AC and PY values.

Examples of alternative arrangements in *title line 3* are:

- 2021-Q1

- 2020-03..2021-02
- 2020 AC and PL
- 2021 AC&FC and PY
- 2018..2020 AC, 2021..2023 PL   or: 2018..23 AC&PL   or: 2018..23
- 2020 AC and PL and ΔPL   or: 2020 AC and PL   or: 2020

Keep it clear and easy to understand – too many elements tend to be confusing. In many cases the information depicted in column headers of tables and legends of data series in charts are sufficient and give better and quicker insight than long texts in *title line 3*. In any case, IBCS rules for abbreviating time periods and dates (see UN 1.2) as well as the rules for abbreviating scenarios and variances must be followed.

In general, position *page titles* at the very upper left corner of a page, directly underneath the message (if a message exists), see Figure UN 2.2-1. Alternatively, position them at the same height as the message if there is not enough space – preferably on the left hand side of the message. The exact position and notation of titles may vary from organization to organization but should be consistent across a single organization.

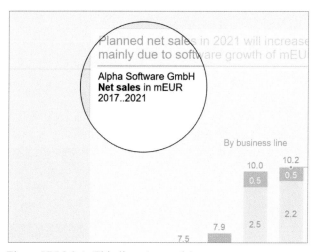

Figure UN 2.2-1: Title lines (example)

Here are some typical examples of *page titles*:

- Chocolate Corp.
  Gross profit in mUSD
  2020

- Construction Inc., Division EMEA
  Net sales in mEUR, **profit margin** in %
  2020-Q3 (AC, PL)

- Beverage Corporation
  Product market portfolio
  2019 and 2020

- Milk & Cheese Corp.
  Shipments in t, by product, by country
  2021-01..10

SUBTITLES

Subtitles identify either page segments or objects (e.g. charts and tables) within a page with multiple objects. They complement the identification information already given in the page title. Subtitles display identifiers that differ from object to object on a page. Put identifiers that are identical for all objects of a page in the page title and not in the subtitles.

In most cases, one line is sufficient for subtitles because different elements of only one dimension have to be identified. Typical examples are:

- **Revenue** in mEUR | **Sales** in SKU | **Avg. price** in EUR/SKU
- Apples | Pears | Oranges
- 2017..2020 | 2021-Q1..Q3 | 2021-10..12

Subtitles are positioned above the respective objects (charts, tables, etc.) which they identify – either centered or left-aligned, see Figure UN 2.2-2.

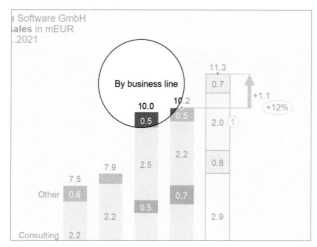

Figure UN 2.2-2: Subtitle (example)

TITLES ON SCREEN PAGES

Unlike titles on printed pages, the layout of titles on screen pages can depend on the aspect ratio and resolution of the device (responsive design). For small devices in landscape format e.g. writing the three title lines in one line separated by a "|" (pipe sign) is a valid solution.

Titles on screen pages can also mutually interfere with interactive navigation objects such as drop-down boxes for selection and check boxes for filtering. Hide these navigation objects when they are not in use or when the screen page is being printed.

UN 2.3 UNIFY THE POSITION OF LEGENDS AND LABELS

A standardized notation of *legends* and *labels* will improve legibility and speed up comprehension of charts, see Figure UN 2.3.

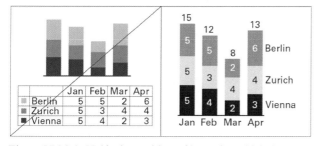

Figure UN 2.3: Unify the position of legends and labels

Legends

Legends (also called "*data series labels*") identify data series.

If possible, integrate legends into charts, not positioned externally. Write legends horizontally for better legibility.

Legends for single column charts and single bar charts are best integrated into the title.

In stacked column charts, position legends either to the left of the leftmost column or to the right of the rightmost column, see Figure UN 2.3-1.

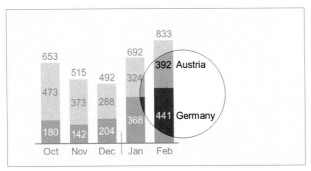

Figure UN 2.3-1: Legends of a stacked column chart (example)

Center legends of stacked bar charts above the top bar, see Figure UN 2.3-2.

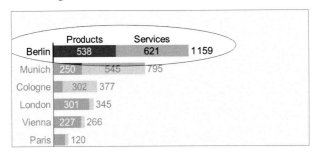

Figure UN 2.3-2: Legends of a stacked bar chart (example)

Assisting lines can help to assign the legends to the correct *visualization elements*. In grouped column charts and grouped bar charts, assisting lines can also help to assign the legends to the correct *visualization elements*, see Figure UN 2.3-3.

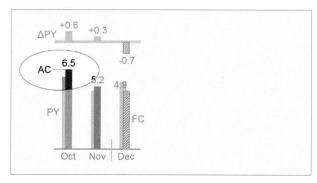

Figure UN 2.3-3: Legend with assisting line (example)

In line charts, position legends either to the right of the line end or close to the course of the line, see Figure UN 2.3-4.

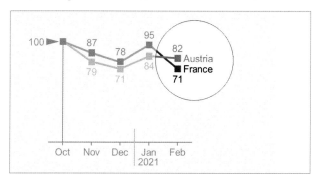

Figure UN 2.3-4: Legends of a line chart (example)

For charts with two value axes, externally positioned legends next to symbols can be a good choice, see Figure UN 2.3-5. When helpful, integrate these legends into the chart by positioning them next to typical points or bubbles.

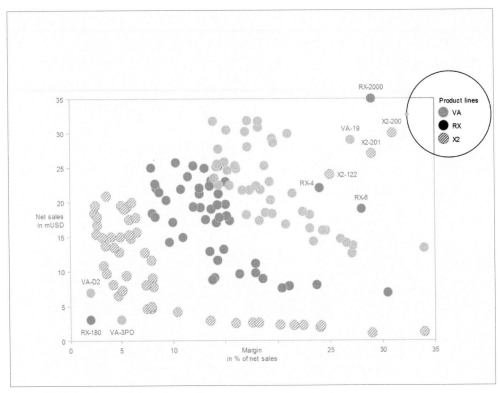

Figure UN 2.3-5: Legends in a chart with two value axes (example)

Labels

Labels (more precise: *data labels*) assign the data values to the respective visualization elements.

Omit labels of small visualization elements, use labels with not more than three digits, and avoid unnecessary and distracting labels (see also the SIMPLIFY rules SI 5 "Avoid distracting details").

Write labels horizontally for better legibility.

Position labels next to their visualization elements. If this is not possible, use lines connecting the labels to the correct visualization elements.

In charts with horizontal category axes, position labels above or below the visualization elements, see Figure UN 2.3-6 and Figure UN 2.3-7. In stacked columns, either center labels in the data points (if the data points are large enough) or position them outside of the data points.

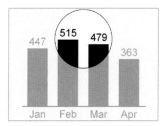

Figure UN 2.3-6: Labels in a column chart (example)

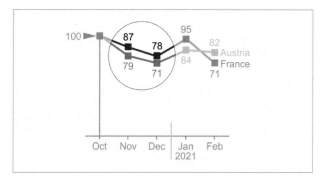

Figure UN 2.3-7: Labels in a line chart (example)

In charts with vertical category axes, position labels right or left of the visualization elements. In stacked bars, either center labels in the data points (if the data points are large enough) or position them outside of the data points, see Figure UN 2.3-8.

Figure UN 2.3-8: Labels in a chart with vertical category axis (example)

In charts with two value axes, position labels next to the visualization elements (above or below, right or left), see Figure UN 2.3-9. Large bubble visualization elements labels can also have centered labels.

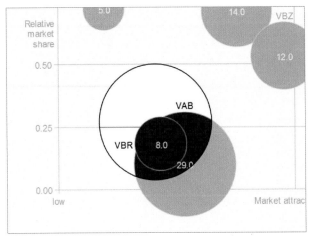

Figure UN 2.3-9: Labels in a chart with two value axes (example)

UN 2.4 UNIFY COMMENTS

Mainly in static reports, *comments* detail other elements (e.g. definitions of data series) and objects such as charts and tables. Sometimes comments also refer to complete pages.

The level of comprehension increases when comments refer directly to the visual representation. Therefore, comments on an object (e.g. chart) are integrated into that object when possible. Comment elements should be linked to the content of tables, charts, etc. through consistently designed comment references (see also SAY rule SA 4.4 "Name sources and link comments"), see Figure UN 2.4-1.

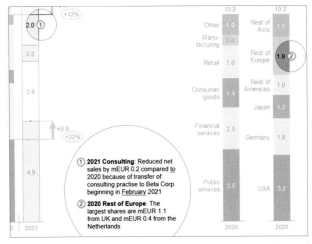

Figure UN 2.4-1: Comments and comment references (example)

UN 2.5 UNIFY FOOTNOTES

Footnotes provide general explanations, explanations of abbreviations, and information that increases the credibility of the content such as the sources or the dates of retrieval and printing. With presentations they can be omitted from slides projected on the wall, but must be included in written material.

Position footnotes at the bottom of a page, see Figure UN 2.5-1.

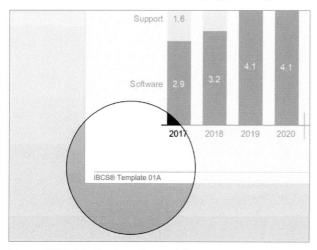

Figure UN 2.5-1: Footnote (example)

UN 3 UNIFY DIMENSIONS

Data in reports, presentations, and dashboards can be viewed from various perspectives called *dimensions*. For example, all business measures, such as sales, profit, margin, etc., constitute a measure dimension, all months, quarters, years, etc., a time dimension. Identifying dimensions via uniform visualization will help with understanding.

This section suggests visualization standards for measures, scenarios, time periods, and structure dimensions.

UN 3.1 UNIFY MEASURES

Business *measures* such as sales, profit, margin, etc. describe, report, and calculate business situations. A standardized notation will help to comprehend the specific characteristics of measures, e.g. whether they are basic measures or calculated ratios of measures, whether they represent value or volume figures, flow or stock figures, or whether they have a positive or negative impact, see Figure UN 3.1.

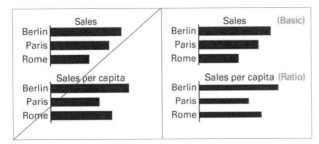

Figure UN 3.1: Unify measures

The *visualization* of business measures is presented here. Their *definition*, generally given in accounting manuals or similar documentation, is *not* discussed here. For the *unified wording* of business measures and their abbreviations see the UNIFY rule UN 1.1 "Unify terms and abbreviations".

BASIC MEASURES AND RATIOS

Basic measures such as "export sales" are directly derived from business processes. *Ratios* such as "return on sales" are quotients of two basic measures.

Basic measures

Basic measures have either *currency units* (e.g. EUR) or *physical units* (e.g. kg). They are neither shares of something (percentages) nor quotients of two measures.

The total width of a category in column charts and bar charts is composed by the width of the columns or bars and the space between them. Set the width of columns or bars showing basic measures as 2/3 of the category width. As long as there is only a single column or bar in a category, the space is then 1/3 of the category width as shown in Figure UN 3.1-1.

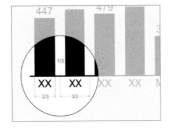

Figure UN 3.1-1: Monthly basic measures in a column chart (example)

Use thick lines for representing basic measures in *line charts*, see Figure UN 3.1-2.

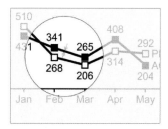

Figure UN 3.1-2: Monthly basic measures in a line chart (example)

Ratios

Ratios are quotients of two basic measures such as "return on sales". In practice, few denominators exist: "Sales", "units sold", "headcount", and "capital" constitute the majority of all business ratios.

If both the enumerator and denominator have the same unit the resulting ratio has no unit. It is expressed in *percent* (e.g. "profit in % of sales").

In addition, if both enumerator and denominator have the same basic measure (e.g. "headcount"), it is called a *share* (e.g. "gender share").

The width of both bars and columns representing *ratios* is half the width of bars and columns representing *basic measures* i.e. 1/3 of the category width, see Figure UN 3.1-3.

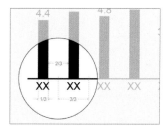

Figure UN 3.1-3: Monthly ratios in a column chart (example)

Represent ratios in *line charts* with thin lines (50% of thick lines), see Figure UN 3.1-4.

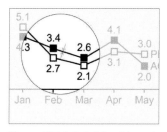

Figure UN 3.1-4: Monthly ratios in a line chart (example)

OTHER MEASURE TYPES

Visually understanding and entire chart without reading any labels requires a comprehensive concept for the visualization of measures or at least measure types. Viewers should be able to see what *content* (e.g. revenues, costs, headcounts, inventory) they are looking at, whether it is a *value* measure such as "profit" or a *volume* measure such as "shipment", whether it's a *flow* measure like "net sales" or a *stock* measure like "inventory" and whether it has a *positive*, *negative*, or *neutral* impact to an organization's goals.

A future version of IBCS will probably address this topic.

UN 3.2 **UNIFY SCENARIOS**

Scenarios (also called data categories, data types, or versions) represent different layers of a business model. Typical scenarios are "Actual", "Previous year", "Plan", "Budget", and "Forecast". In special cases *benchmarks* such as competitor data or market averages are also called scenarios.

Often comparisons and variances between different scenarios are presented to provide business insights.

There are two basic types of scenarios:

1   **Actual scenarios** refer to *measured* data about things that already happened in present or past time periods. The terms we use most often for scenarios of this type are 'Actual' and 'Previous year' (meaning actual data from previous year).

2   **Planned scenarios** refer to *fictitious* (not materialized) data. The terms we use most often for scenarios of this type are 'Plan' and 'Budget'.

In-between those two basic scenario types there is a third one:

3   **Forecasted scenarios** refer to *expected* data which are strictly speaking fictitious but already taking into account measured data. A typical example for expected data is the sales forecast based on the measured order entry. Forecasted scenarios represent a higher level of certainty than scenarios with planned data but are not completely materialized yet. The term we use most often for scenarios of this type is 'Forecast'.

When analyzing charts and tables, it is very important to quickly recognize whether you look at measured, expected, or fictitious data. Readers of IBCS compliant reports can visually recognize these scenario types by looking at the *area fill* of a visualization element without having to read the labels. Typical chart visualization elements such as bars, columns, line chart markers, scenario triangles, etc. carry the semantic scenario notation.

In charts presenting variances, their *axes* carry the semantic scenario notation in order to show the respective reference scenario (see UN 4.1).

In charts with stacked columns, stacked areas, and charts with multiple lines or areas, the application of this semantic scenario notation can become a challenge. Apply the scenario notation to the lowest segment and fill all upper segments with different shades of gray. Add a frame (outlined) or hatch pattern to these segments if they represent planned or forecasted data.

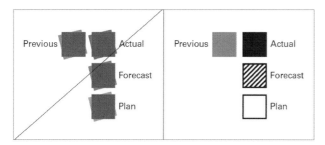

Figure UN 3.2: Unify scenarios

ACTUAL SCENARIOS: MEASURED DATA

Scenarios with measured data are identified by a solid dark (e.g. dark gray) fill for the areas of the respective visualization elements.

If measured data of recent periods ("Actual") are compared with measured data from earlier periods (e.g. "Previous year", "Previous month'", "Month YoY") in a scenario comparison, then the areas representing the earlier periods are presented with a lighter solid fill (e.g. light gray).

Note: If data from multiple periods is presented in a time series there is no need for coloring earlier periods with a lighter fill.

Use consistent abbreviations for "Actual" and for previous periods such as "Previous Year" across an organization. The two-letter codes "AC" and "PY" work well.

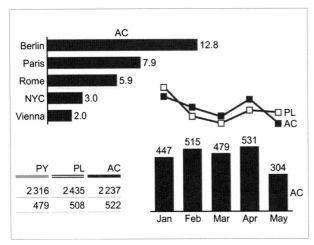

Figure UN 3.2-1: Visualization of measured data (examples)

PLANNED SCENARIOS: FICTITIOUS DATA

Scenarios with fictitious data are identified by outlined (bordered, framed) areas of the respective visualization elements. The areas within these borders literally "fill up when materializing", e.g. when changing from fictitious data to measured data.

Use consistent abbreviations for planned scenarios across an organization. The two-letter codes "PL" for "Plan" and "BU" for "Budget" work well.

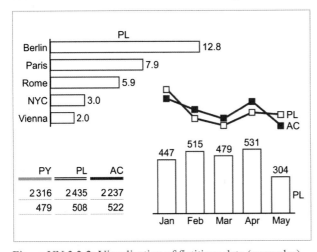

Figure UN 3.2-2: Visualization of fictitious data (examples)

FORECASTED SCENARIOS: EXPECTED DATA

Expected data is strictly speaking fictitious, so they are also identified by outlined areas. However, as it is based on measured data, the area fill of the respective visualization elements becomes hatched. The color of the dark stripes correspond to the color of measured data (e.g. dark gray).

Use consistent abbreviations for forecasted scenarios across an organization. "FC" for "Forecast" works well.

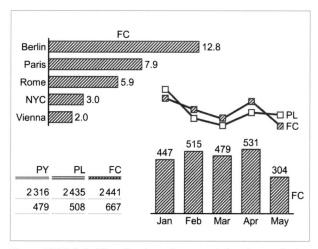

Figure UN 3.2-3: Visualization of expected data (examples)

UN 3.3 UNIFY TIME PERIODS, USE HORIZONTAL AXES

Using standard notations for *time periods* (for flow measures) and *points of time* (for stock measures) is important as they are frequently applied to all forms of business communication. This requires standard notations for the visual direction of time, time period and points of time abbreviations and – in charts with horizontal time axes – category widths, see Figure UN 3.3.

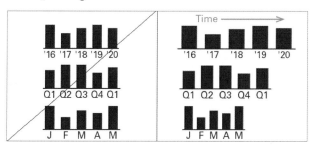

Figure UN 3.3: Unify time periods, use horizontal axes

VISUAL DIRECTION OF TIME PERIODS

As opposed to structural comparisons, visualize data series over time with horizontal axes. In tables, present data series over time in columns. In both cases time moves from left to right, see Figure UN 3.3-1.

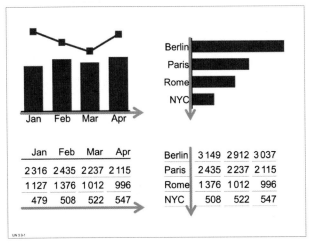

Figure UN 3.3-1: Visualization of time vs. structure (examples)

TIME PERIOD AND POINTS OF TIME ABBREVIATIONS

For a better understanding, use unified *abbreviations for time periods and points in time* within an organization. The pattern YYYY-MM-DD (e.g. 2021-06-29) as recommended by ISO 8601 is a good choice for time periods for its unambiguousness and easy sorting. The *abbreviations* in Figure UN 3.3-2 also work well:

	Abbreviations		
Time periods	Long	Short	Within year
Year	2021	'21	
Quarter	2021-Q2	'21-Q2	Q2
Month	2021-01	'21-01	Jan
	Jan 2021	Jan '21	Jan
Week	2021-W37	'21-W37	W37
Day	2021-06-29	'21-06-29	Jun 29
	Jun 29, 2021	Jun 29 '21	Jun 29

Figure UN 3.3-2: Abbreviations for time periods (example)

In some countries or organizations other abbreviations are common. They can also be applied as long as they are used consistently.

A "." (full-stop) before the period name is a good choice to indicate the *first day* of a time period, e.g. ".2021" for the first day of 2021 or ".Jun" for the first day of June.

Likewise, appending "." (full-stop) to the period name can visualize the *last day* of a time period, e.g. "2021." for the last day of 2021 or "Jun." for the last day of June.

The sign ".." (two full-stops) is a good choice to indicate a *time span,* e.g. "Jan..Mar" (without blanks) for "from January to March." N.B.: Use two dots instead of three dots ("ellipsis").

CATEGORY WIDTHS

When helpful, differentiate different types of time periods with different *category widths* according to this rule: the longer the period the wider the category segments on the category axis, see Figure UN 3.3-3.

When labeling stacked columns the category segments might be somewhat wider, while in case of charts with many columns and restricted space they might be rather narrow. In any case, if certain period types have been allocated certain category widths, this allocation should be the same at least for an entire page of a report or a screen of a dashboard..

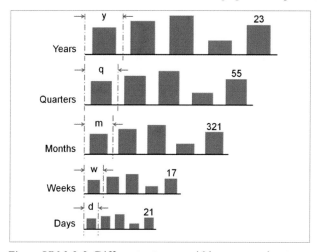

Figure UN 3.3-3: Different category widths representing types of time periods (conceptual)

UN 3.4 UNIFY STRUCTURE DIMENSIONS, USE VERTICAL AXES

Structure dimensions are all dimensions that are *not* measures, scenarios, or time periods. In many cases, the following structure dimensions are used: regions, organization units, products, customers, channels, and accounts.

In general, display structures on vertical category axes. There are few exceptions to this rule where (de facto) standards require other data than time series to be presented on horizontal axes (e.g. statistical representations such as bell curves). Use custom symbols if it is helpful to differentiate structure dimensions, see Figure UN 3.4.

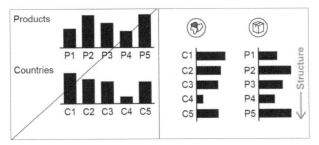

Figure UN 3.4: Unify structure dimensions, use vertical axes

UN 4   UNIFY ANALYSES

Analyses are carried out in order to understand certain business situations, e.g. finding the greatest variances from a plan or calculating the monthly average.

This section comprises analyses regarding different dimensions such as scenario analyses, time series analyses, and structure analyses. A section covering different adjustment analyses is added.

UN 4.1   UNIFY SCENARIO ANALYSES

Analyze *scenarios* by comparing them and by calculating their absolute and relative variances. Notation standards for scenario analyses cover the labelling of variances and the semantic design of chart elements such as columns, bars, and axes, see Figure UN 4.1.

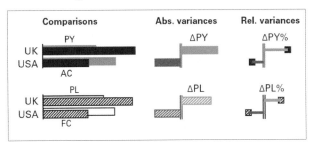

Figure UN 4.1: Unify scenario analyses

SCENARIO COMPARISONS

Scenario comparisons place the data of different scenarios next to each other, for example actual data next to previous year or budget data. This is relevant for both charts and tables. In tables, scenarios usually are shown in columns.

When comparing, arrange scenarios of *different time periods* (mainly years) in temporal ascending order either from left to right (horizontal axes) or from above to below (vertical axes), e.g. PY (= AC 2020), FC 2021, PL 2022.

The order sequence of scenarios referring to the identical time period – e.g. PL 2021, FC 2021, AC 2021 is defined by the time when the scenarios are created.

In case of comparing measured data of different time periods in a scenario comparison, use the scenario labels (e.g. AC and PY) rather than the labels of the time periods (e.g. 2021 and 2020) in both charts and tables. Make sure that the time period necessary to interpret the scenarios is clearly set in the title, a legend or a column header.

Scenario comparisons are visualized either by overlapped grouping of columns or bars (e.g. overlapping columns of PY and AC or overlapping bars of PL and AC), or with *scenario triangles* using the respective area coding (e.g. solid light color for PY) to represent the reference scenario, see Figure UN 4.1-1 and Figure UN 4.1-2. *Scenario triangles* can also be added to overlapped bars or columns in order to show a third scenario.

The scenarios AC and FC stand in the foreground of other scenarios in grouped columns or bars.

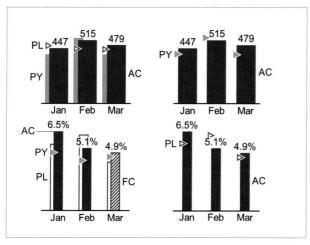

Figure UN 4.1-1: Column charts with scenario comparisons (examples)

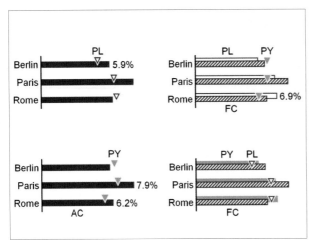

Figure UN 4.1-2: Bar charts with scenario comparisons (examples)

ABSOLUTE VARIANCES

An *absolute variance* is the difference between two values of one measure from different scenarios.

Use consistent signs and abbreviations for absolute variances across an organization. It's a good choice to represent the absolute variance with the sign "Δ" as a prefix to the subtrahend of the respective difference, i.e. "ΔPL" for the absolute difference "AC minus PL" (AC-PL) or – if FC is compared to PL – "FC minus PL" (FC-PL).

The most common *absolute variances* are the following:

- **Plan variance:** "ΔPL" for AC-PL or FC-PL (when comparing FC to PL)
- **Previous year variance:** "ΔPY" for AC-PY or FC-PY (when comparing FC to PY)

If it is not clear whether AC or FC is compared to plan in ΔPL or ΔPY, use the following notation:

- **Plan variance:** "AC-PL" and "FC-PL"
- **Previous year variance**: "AC-PY" and "FC-PY"

Positive absolute variances (same as positive percent variances) have a "+" to emphasis this aspect: "+13" always means a *variance* of 13, "13" means any absolute value of 13.

If absolute variances are displayed in columns or bars ("variance columns" or "variance bars"), these variance columns or bars have the same width and the same scale as the corresponding base value columns or bars.

Variance bars and columns representing a *positive impact* on business issues (mainly result) are colored green, those representing a *negative impact* red, see Figure UN 4.1-3. Variance bars and columns representing a *neutral impact* are colored blue. If no color is available, replace red with dark gray, green with light gray and blue with medium gray. For readers with color deficiency, replace green with blue-green.

If it is helpful, numbers in tables representing variances are colored in the same way.

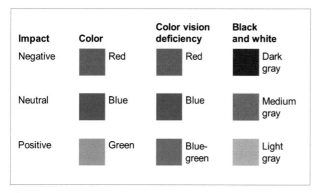

Figure UN 4.1-3: Colors for displaying variances (conceptual)

Note: These colors for positive, negative, or neutral variances must not be confused with red and green "traffic lights" (see also EXPRESS rule EX 2.5 "Replace traffic lights").

In order to visualize the *scenario to be analyzed* (minuend), apply scenario notation to the fill of the variance columns or bars, e.g. *solid* green or red fill for AC and *hatched* green or red fill for FC, see Figure UN 4.1-4. If in special cases the minuend is PL (e.g. variance of plan versus average) the variance columns and bars are *outlined* green or red.

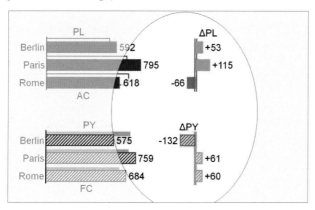

Figure UN 4.1-4: Bar charts with absolute variances (examples)

Position data labels for variance columns and bars always *outside* of these visualization elements. These labels' position aligns with the direction of positive or negative increase, i.e. the label of a positive variance (increase) in a variance column is positioned above the column; the label of a negative variance (decrease) in a variance bar on the left-hand side outside of the bar.

In order to visualize the *reference scenario* (subtrahend) of an absolute variance (in general PY, PL, or BU), apply scenario notation to the axis: For absolute variances to PY the axis is colored solid light, for absolute variances to PL or BU the axis takes an outline shape (two parallel lines).

Treat variances of ratios, e.g. percent values (profit on sales) in a special way: Absolute variances of percent values are called *percent points*, e.g. AC 50% - PL 40% = +10pp.

RELATIVE VARIANCES

A *relative variance* is an absolute variance as a percentage of the subtrahend of the absolute variance.

Use consistent signs and abbreviations for relative variances across an organization. It's a good choice to use the sign "Δ" as a prefix to the subtrahend and the sign "%" as appendix, e.g. ΔPL% for the relative variance (AC-PL)/PL*100.

The most common *relative variances* are the following:

- **Plan variance**: "ΔPL%" for (AC-PL)/PL*100 or (FC-PL)/PL*100 (when comparing FC to PL)
- **Previous year variance**: "ΔPY%" for (AC-PY)/PY*100 or (FC-PY)/PY*100 (when comparing FC to PY)

Display "n.a." (not available) if the calculated relative variance cannot be interpreted, as is often the case when a positive value is compared to a negative reference value (denominator):

Profit AC = 30
Profit PL = -30
ΔPL = +60
ΔPL% = 60 / -30 = -200% => n.a.

Use the following notation, if it is not clear whether AC or FC is compared to Plan:

- **Plan variance**: "(AC-PL)%" and "(FC-PL)%"
- **Previous year variance**: "(AC-PY)%" and "(FC-PY)%"

Positive relative variances (same as positive absolute variances) have a "+"-to emphasize this aspect: "+13%" always means a *variance* of 13%, "13%" means any kind of percentage such as ratio or a share.

Relative variances are displayed in thin columns (vertical pins) or thin bars (horizontal pins), see Figure UN 4.1-5 and Figure UN 4.1-6.

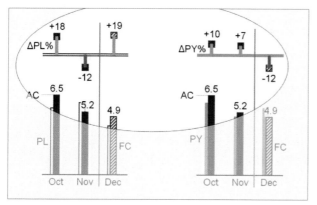

Figure UN 4.1-5: Columns charts with relative variances (examples)

Pins representing a *positive impact* on business issues (mainly result) are colored green, those representing a *negative impact* red. Pins representing a *neutral impact* on business issues are colored blue. If no color is available, replace red with dark gray, green with light gray and blue with medium gray. For readers with color deficiency, replace green with blue-green.

Position data labels of pins outside the pin in the direction of the positive or negative increase, e.g. position the label of a horizontal pin depicting "sales growth in %" (green) on the right hand side of the pin, position the label of a vertical pin depicting "cost decrease in %" (green) below the pin.

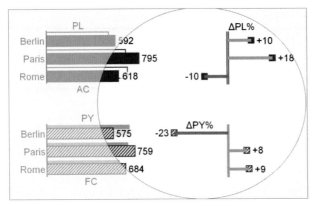

Figure UN 4.1-6: Bar charts with relative variances (examples)

Add head markers to the pins to visualize the *scenario to be analyzed* (minuend). Apply the scenario notation to the fill of the heads, e.g. solid dark fill for AC and hatched fill for FC.

Apply the scenario notation to the axis in order to visualize the *reference scenario* for a relative variance (in general PY, PL, or BU): For relative variances to PY fill the axis solid light, for relative variances to PL or BU the axis takes an outline shape (two parallel lines).

Treat relative variances of percent values the same way as relative variances of absolute values, e.g. (AC 50% - PL 40%) / PL 40% * 100 = +25%.

UN 4.2 UNIFY TIME SERIES ANALYSES

Use a consistent notation for *time series analyses* such as year-to-date analyses, moving analyses, and temporal indexing within an organization. The suggestions depicted in Figure UN 4.2 and explained in the following paragraphs work well.

Analyses	Symbol	Example	Application
Difference	x - y	AC'20 - AC'19	"Year to date"
Time span	a..b	Feb..Jun'21	_Jan _Feb _Mar
Year to date	_x	_Jun'21	123 234 546
Year to go	x_	Jun'21_	22 46 86
Rolling	_x	_Jun'21	
Average	ø	ø'21	
First day	.x	.Aug'21	
Last day	x.	Aug.'21	J F M A M

Figure UN 4.2: Unify time series analyses

YEAR-TO-DATE ANALYSES

Year-to-date analyses (YTD) refer to the period from the beginning of the year to the present (*YTD time span*). The beginning of the year is not necessarily January 1. Some companies have fiscal years beginning at other dates.

Where helpful, visualize analyses showing YTD values by prefixing an underscore to the *time period name*, e.g. "_Jun 2021", see Figure UN 4.2-1. Optionally, add the first period of the YTD time span, e.g. "January_June 2021". In charts, add the underscores as a prefix at the left hand side of the end of the columns or at the upper side of the end of bars.

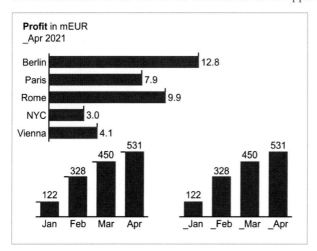

Figure UN 4.2-1: Year-to-date labeling in a column chart (example)

Year-to-date operations cover accumulation of values, calculation of averages, and picking of last date values.

- YTD accumulation

In this context, *accumulation* means totaling successive time period values from the beginning of a calendar year or fiscal year to the present. In this stricter sense, accumulation applies only to flow measures, such as sales or costs.

If it is helpful, visualize analyses showing *YTD accumulation* with the underscore prefix (without additional notation) e.g. "_Jun 2021".

- YTD average

In this context, the *average* is calculated by dividing the *YTD accumulation* by the number of periods in the *YTD time span*. YTD average applies to both *flow* and *stock measures*.

If it is helpful, visualize analyses showing *YTD averages* with the underscore prefix and an appended "∅" sign, e.g. "_Jun 2021∅".

- Last date value

A special YTD analyses for stock measures is picking the *value of the last date* in the *YTD time span.*

If it is helpful, visualize analyses showing *last date values* with the underscore prefix and an appended full-stop, e.g. "_Jun 2021.".

YEAR-TO-GO ANALYSES

By analogy to year-to-date analyses, *year-to-go analyses* (YTG) refer to the period from the presence (now) to the end of the (fiscal) year.

Where helpful, visualize analyses showing YTG values by appending an underscore to the *time period name*, e.g. "Jun 2021_".

MOVING ANALYSES

In general, *moving analyses* refer to the period of the previous twelve months.

If it is helpful, visualize moving analyses by prefixing the *time period name* with a tilde, e.g. "~Jun 2021" or "~Jun∅" respectively, see Figure UN 4.2-2. In charts, add the tilde as a prefix at the left hand side of the end of columns or the upper side of the end of bars.

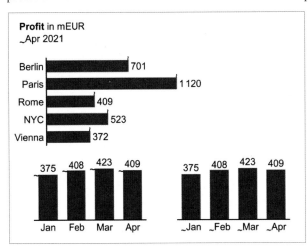

Figure UN 4.2-2: Moving analysis labeling in a column chart (example)

Similar to year-to-date operations, moving analyses cover accumulation of values (*moving annual total* MAT), calculation of averages (*moving annual average* MAA), and picking of last date values.

The visualization concept for *accumulation of values*, *calculation of averages*, and *picking of last date values* is identical to the visualization concept of year-to-date analyses – the tilde simply replaces the underscore.

TEMPORAL INDEXING

Using *temporal indexing* (*indexing a time series*), all period values are depicted in relation to the value of a chosen reference period (1 or 100%).

To visualize temporal indexing, position a black arrowhead pointing right at the left of the index point. "100%" or "100" is written left of the arrowhead, see Figure UN 4.2-3. If helpful, add an assisting horizontal line.

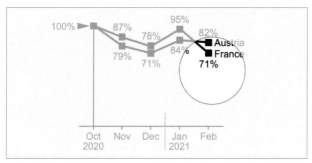

Figure UN 4.2-3: Visualizing temporal indexing (example)

UN 4.3 UNIFY STRUCTURE ANALYSES

Notation for *structure analyses* covers averaging, ranking, selecting, indexing, and normalizing.

STRUCTURAL AVERAGE

The term "*average*" usually refers to the mean of different values. The section on time series analyses described *temporal averages* (e.g. monthly average of a year). *Structural averages* (e.g. average sales of several subsidiaries) are covered here. Typical structural averages are average by product, average by country, and average by customer.

Visualize analyses showing structural averages with a "∅" sign either appended or as a prefix, e.g. "Europe∅" or "∅464", see Figure UN 4.3-1. If needed, add an assisting line.

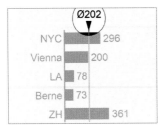

Figure UN 4.3-1: Visualizing structural averaging (example)

RANKING

Ranking analyses refer to descending or ascending rankings of structure elements. Words can be ranked in alphabetical order, numbers in numerical order.

If helpful, append an arrow sign to rankings, e.g. "country names↓" or "product sales↑".

SELECTING

The structure analysis *selecting* is related to the structure analysis *ranking*, used, in general, to determine either maximal (fastest, most expensive) elements or the minimal (slowest, cheapest) elements. Top ten, last ten, first quartile, last percentile, etc., are common forms of selecting.

A future version of IBCS may address the visualization of the structural analysis *selecting*.

STRUCTURAL INDEXING

Structural indexing depicts all element values in relation to the value of a chosen reference element (=1 or 100%). Typical reference elements are the mean, the maximum, or a specific element in a given structure, e.g. "Germany = 100%".

To visualize *structural indexing*, position a black arrowhead close to the index point. "100%" or "100", is written next to the arrowhead, see Figure UN 4.3-2. If helpful, add an assisting line.

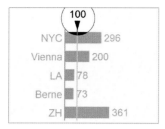

Figure UN 4.3-2: Visualizing structural indexing (example)

STRUCTURAL NORMALIZING

Structural normalizing refers to the comparison of several shares of some whole, e.g. shares of export to different countries. Indexing and normalizing are similar analyses, indexing refers to one element (e.g. a selected country), normalizing to the whole of several parts (e.g. country sales in % of Europe sales).

To visualize *structural normalizing*, add an assisting line representing 100%, see Figure UN 4.3-3. Position a black arrowhead at one end of the assisting line. "100%" or "100", is written next to the arrowhead.

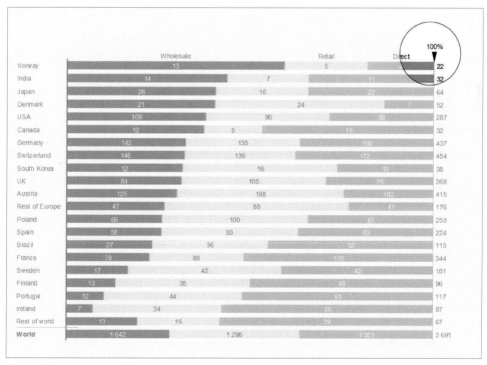

Figure UN 4.3-3: Visualizing structural normalizing (example)

UN 4.4 UNIFY ADJUSTMENT ANALYSES

Adjustment analyses can offer insight into root causes as they adjust values by neutralizing special effects. In general, *adjustment analyses* are used in conjunction with scenario analyses. Here the values of one scenario are recalculated with correction factors from another scenario: e.g., adjust AC sales for currency effects by re-measuring them with the PY exchange rates.

Typical *adjustment analyses* deal with currency, inflation, and seasonal effects.

A future version of IBCS may create a visualization concept for *adjustment analyses*.

UN 5 UNIFY INDICATORS

Indicators in reports and presentations serve different purposes, e.g. highlighting and scaling. Using the indicator with the same design for the same purpose will help to identify the situation much faster.

UN 5.1 UNIFY HIGHLIGHTING INDICATORS

The message to be conveyed should be highlighted on the respective page by appropriate visual means. *Highlighting elements* enhance the meaning and importance of other elements. Within an organization use consistently designed highlighting elements for *assisting* purposes, for visualizing *differences* and *trends*, for underlining *values*, for indicating a *reference*, or for linking *comments,* see Figure UN 5.1.

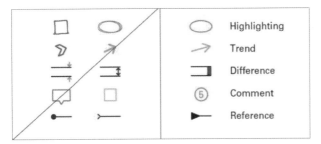

Figure UN 5.1: Unify highlighting indicators

ASSISTING LINES AND AREAS

Using *assisting lines* works well for different highlighting purposes, e.g. for showing differences, for separating, arranging, or grouping data in charts or tables, or for coordinating visualization elements of different charts, see Figure UN 5.1-1.

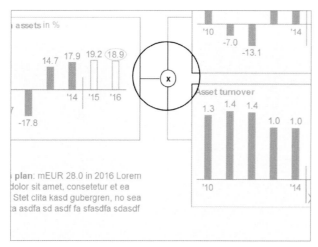

assets in %

14.7 17.9 19.2 (18.9)

'14 '15 '16

-17.8

x

'10
-7.0

'14

-13.1

Asset turnover

1.3 1.4 1.4

1.0 1.0

'10 '14

plan: mEUR 28.0 in 2016 Lorem
dolor sit amet, consetetur et ea
Stet clita kasd gubergren, no sea
a asdfa sd asdf fa sfasdfa sdasdf

Figure UN 5.1-1: Assisting lines (example)

Using *assisting areas* works well for e.g. highlighting words in a longer text or highlighting certain parts of charts or tables.

DIFFERENCE MARKERS

Highlight differences in charts by using two parallel assisting lines to project the respective lengths of two columns or bars to consistently designed *difference markers* highlighting the distance between the two assisting lines.

Position difference markers in a way that they can clearly highlight the respective difference, see Figure UN 5.1-2.

Difference markers representing a positive impact on business issues (e.g. profit) are colored green; difference markers representing a negative impact on business issues (e.g. loss) are colored red. Difference markers representing neutral impacts on business issues are colored blue. You can add an arrowhead if you also want to highlight whether the difference represents an increase or decrease.

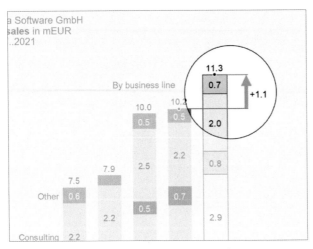

Figure UN 5.1-2: Difference markers (example)

TREND ARROWS

Consistently designed arrows can highlight trends in charts and (seldom) tables, too.

Position *trend arrows* in a way that they can clearly highlight the direction of the trend with the respective slope, see Figure UN 5.1-3. The arrow starts at the first period and ends at the last period included in the calculation of the respective trend. The arrowhead is pointing in time direction. Adding a number and a designation for the calculation method (e.g. CAGR: 10.8%) will give additional insight.

Trend arrows representing a positive trend are colored green; trend arrows representing a negative impact on business issues (e.g. loss) are colored red. Trend arrows representing neutral impacts on business issues are colored blue.

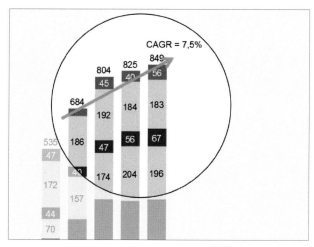

Figure UN 5.1-3: Trend arrow (example)

HIGHLIGHTING ELLIPSES

Use consistently designed means for highlighting single values. *Highlighting ellipses* are a good choice, see Figure UN 5.1-4. Good reasons for highlighting single values are e.g.

- **Highlighting messages**: If the message refers to a specific value in a chart, table or graph, highlight this value with a blue ellipse.
- **Highlighting additional values**: Sometimes it is helpful to add additional values (e.g. percent value) in charts or tables.

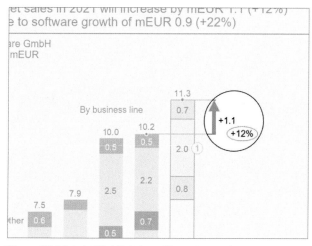

Figure UN 5.1-4: Highlighting ellipse (example)

REFERENCE ARROWHEADS

Use consistently designed *reference arrowheads* for highlighting a reference standard. Examples of reference standards are:

- **Indices**: Either one value (e.g. the value of the year 2017) is set to 100%, or the total is set to 100% (see sections about time series analyses and structure analyses).
- **Benchmarks**: Popular benchmarks are market averages, competitors, or best practices.

Position the arrowhead close to the point representing the index or the benchmark, see Figure UN 5.1-5. Write the label for the index (e.g. "100%" or "100") or for the benchmark (e.g. "Market avg.") next to the arrowhead. The arrowhead points in the direction of an imaginary index or benchmark line. If helpful, add an assisting line.

Figure UN 5.1-5: Reference arrowhead (example)

COMMENT REFERENCES

Use consistently designed *comment references* in pairs to link comments to the corresponding values or positions in a chart or a table (see also SAY rule SA 4.4 "Name sources and link comments"), see Figure UN 5.1-6.

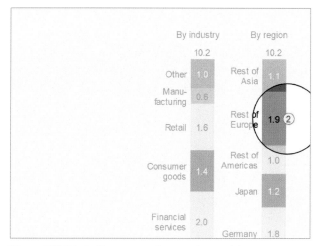

Figure UN 5.1-6: Comment reference (example)

OTHER HIGHLIGHTING INDICATORS

Add visualization elements for not-valid values, limits, or other relevant phenomena. Standardize and document these "signals" so that they become an effective means of communication.

UN 5.2 UNIFY SCALING INDICATORS

Proper *scaling* is very important for the creation of meaningful charts. Several semantic *scaling indicators* exist to deal with in challenging scaling problems. Use *scaling lines* and *scale bands)* if necessary, see Figure UN 5.2.

A future version of IBCS may suggest additional visualization concepts for *scaling*.

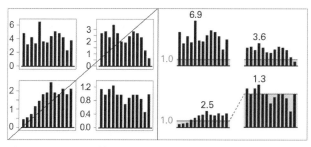

Figure UN 5.2: Unify scaling indicators

SCALING LINES

Use scaling lines when comparing multiple charts (with the same unit) having different scales. Position a scaling line parallel to the category axis at the same numerical height in all charts, see Figure UN 5.2-1. If one chart among several other charts uses a different scale, this fact can easily be identified (in general, the differing scale uses a multiplier of ten).

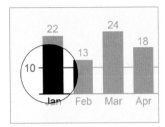

Figure UN 5.2-1: Scaling line (example)

SCALE BANDS

If helpful, fill the areas between the scaling lines and the category axes with light color, see Figure UN 5.2-2.

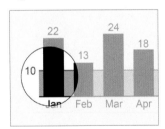

Figure UN 5.2-2: Scale band (example)

UN 5.3 UNIFY OUTLIER INDICATORS

Sometimes values (mostly relative variances) can be very big in comparison to other values. If such an *outlier* is not important for business, e.g. a big relative variance of a small value, do not scale the whole chart to this outlier rather visualize unimportant outliers with consistently designed *outlier indicators*. It's a good choice to omit the pin head and add *outlier triangles* pointing in the direction of growth, see Figure UN 5.3.

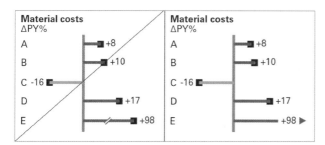

Figure UN 5.3: Unify outlier indicators

CONCEPTUAL RULES

The *conceptual rules* from the SAY (convey a message) and STRUCTURE (organize content) sections of the SUCCESS formula help to clearly relay content by using an appropriate storyline. They are based on the work of authors such as Barbara Minto[9].

---

[9] Minto, Barbara: The Pyramid Principle, 3rd edition, 2002

SAY – CONVEY A MESSAGE

SAY covers all aspects of conveying messages to the recipients of reports.

Conveying messages means that reports, both as a whole as well as within their individual components, intend to say something to the recipients. Messages in this sense can be determinations, explanations, clarifications, recommendations, and other forms of statements.

This chapter covers introducing, delivering, supporting, and summarizing messages with respect to the objectives of senders and receivers.

SA 1 KNOW OBJECTIVES

Good message conveying reports and presentations successfully achieve both the goals of the writer (speaker) and of the readers (audience).

SA 1.1 KNOW OWN GOALS

Do not start creating a report or presentation without a clear vision of what to achieve with it. The least goal is to inform about an interesting detection. A higher goal is to make the reader (audience) understand a problem by explaining it. The ultimate goal is to get a decision on a suggestion provided and to cause corresponding actions.

Figure SA 1.1: Know own goals

SA 1.2 KNOW TARGET AUDIENCE

A good report (presentation) will try to answer the questions of the readers (audience). So it is important to know the target audience (e.g. their function, position, network, knowledge, experience, attitude, behavior, worries, cultural background) and their goals, preferences, and expectations. Do they only want to get informed about interesting detections, or are they looking for an explanation to a problem? Are they willing to make decisions and to act accordingly? Who might object to the message and why?

Figure SA 1.2: Know target audience

SA 2 INTRODUCE MESSAGE

The addressees appreciate an introduction mapping the actual situation followed by an explanation of the given problem. Raising a question will focus on the given message.

SA 2.1 MAP SITUATION

Mapping the situation means compiling and presenting the related facts. Be sure to cover all relevant aspects and obtain a general consensus concerning the facts. In general, this means not yet describing the given problem but presenting facts and goals already known to the reader or audience. It is advisable to begin with a positive or generally accepted description of the situation in order to prevent early contradictions.

Figure SA 2.1: Map situation

SA 2.2 EXPLAIN PROBLEM

After mapping the situation, introduce the challenge or complication, affecting the reader or the audience. It should make everyone aware of an interesting, critical, or even dangerous problem.

Figure SA 2.2: Explain problem

SA 2.3 RAISE QUESTION

A good introduction raises the relevant question from the perspective of the recipient of how to solve the complication in the described situation. The question at the beginning of each report or presentation then leads to the message, i.e. the answer to the question.

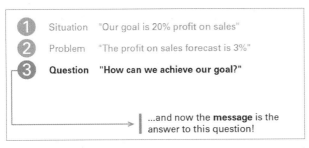

Figure SA 2.3: Raise question

SA 3 DELIVER MESSAGE

Delivering the message means answering the question asked at the end of the introduction. Messages detect, explain, or suggest something the report or presentation later explains in detail.

SA 3.1 DETECT, EXPLAIN, OR SUGGEST

Messages in reports and presentations can detect, evaluate, explain, warn, complain, threaten, excuse, suggest, or recommend something interesting. Make sure to deliver these messages in a complete sentence in order to be understood.

Today, many messages in business reporting are pure *detections*. Since detections are statements that can be checked whether they are true or false, they should be formulated as precisely as possible.

Explaining the reasons for a detection (*explanation*) or even deriving a *suggestion* on how to solve the problem or at least on how to further proceed can add value.

Figure SA 3.1: Detect, explain, or suggest

Figure SA 3.1-1 shows a classification of messages with examples from the business environment.

Detections	Explanations	Suggestions
① **Export** share of PSI sank in Q1 from 45% to 40%	...**because** product approvals are lacking in Asia and America .	**Therefore**, we should move up authorization for the USA to August.
② **Inventory** is replaced 5 times, which is below industry average of 6.5	... **because** suppliers are not particularly reliable.	**Therefore**, we should re-examine the selection of suppliers.
③ **Sales** in spare parts fell by 12%	...**because** competitors are increasingly imitating our products.	**Therefore**, we should redesign our spare parts business.
④ **Personnel costs** in Berlin amount to 35% of sales, which is 6app above the target	...**because** the personnel situation has not been adjusted.	**Therefore**, we should utilize logistics through cooperations.
⑤ **Results** for kitchens in Q1 were 3 million under budget for the first time	...**because** we had a lot of down time at our new plant C.	**Therefore,** we should re-examine the new management concept.
⑥ **Production costs** at C are 11% higher than the average	...**because** lot sizes here are smaller than at all the other plants.	**Therefore**, we should build the planned warehouse already this year.
⑦ **Result** has deteriorated despite a 6% increase in sales	...**because** sales often gave discounts that were too large	**Therefore**, we should reorganize the management of sales.
⑧ **Margins** in films are 5% lower than in the previous year	...**because** excess capacity still exists in Eastern Europe-	**Therefore**, we should not begin production in China as planned.
⑨ **Consulting time** for small customers takes up 50%	...**because** consulting was provided without concrete specifications.	**Therefore**, we should focus consultations on customer potential.

Figure SA 3.1-1: Classification of messages (Source: Hichert, R. and Kornwachs, K.)

SA 3.2 SAY MESSAGE FIRST

Every report, every presentation, and every single page or exhibit can be summed up with a clear overall message. This message usually comes first and is proven afterwards. For the readers or the audience it is more difficult to follow the storyline if the message comes at the end.

Figure SA 3.2: Say message first

Positioning and designing messages consistently as suggested in the UNIFY rule UN 2.1 "Unify messages" will help identify a message being one.

Be cautious applying this rule in presentations (not in reports) with bad, unexpected, or unpleasant messages (e.g. layoffs) or in a cultural environment, where directness is considered impolite.

SA 4 SUPPORT MESSAGE

Supporting the message covers some technical and practical aspects of message conveyance.

SA 4.1 PROVIDE EVIDENCE

Substantiate the message in order to prove the message by facts and figures. If possible, a presentation slide should itself explain or prove the speaker's message and not – as very often seen in practice – be explained by the speaker. This can be done by spoken sentences possibly supported by charts, tables, and pictures.

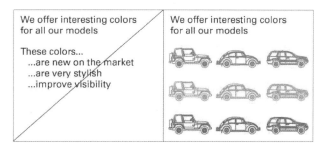

Figure SA 4.1: Provide evidence

SA 4.2 USE PRECISE WORDS

The more unambiguous the language, the clearer the message. Only precise words will be understood. Speaking about "relevant" or "significant" (in common speech, not as a statistical term) content leads to misinterpretations and misunderstandings. Speaking about facts and figures will prevent them.

Figure SA 4.2: Use precise words

The unification of terminology requested in the UNIFY rules UN 1.1 "Unify terms and abbreviations" and UN 1.2 "Unify numbers, units, and dates" will help to achieve such an unambiguous language.

SA 4.3 HIGHLIGHT MESSAGE

Visually highlight messages in the communication objects presented – namely in charts, tables, graphs, and pictures. This facilitates comprehension and reduces the time needed to understand complex situations. In most cases, it should be possible to highlight the important parts of the content by underlining the most important facts or emphasizing interesting details. Objects and pages without highlighting indicators tend to be a statistic rather than a report.

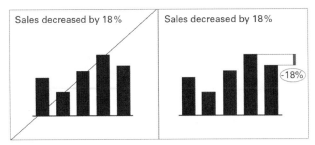

Figure SA 4.3: Highlight message

Using consistent highlighting indicators, as suggested in the UNIFY rule UN 5.1 "Unify highlighting indicators", will help to understand the message better and faster.

SA 4.4 NAME SOURCES

Naming sources for the material presented increases the credibility. Projected slides can omit them but written reports and handouts must include them.

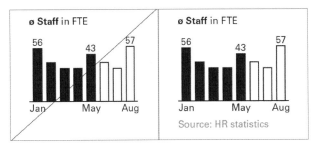

Figure SA 4.4: Name sources

SA 4.5 LINK COMMENTS

Use comments in written reports and handouts to add explanations, conclusions, and similar statements. Projected slides in presentations rarely need any comments because the comments are given by the speaker.

Number comments related to specific parts of a page (e.g. words, numbers, or visualization elements) and link them to the respective parts. Post numbered comments in text boxes on free areas of a page.

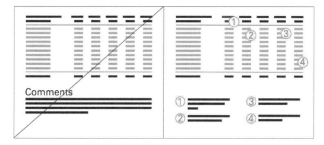

Figure SA 4.5: Link comments

A consistent design of comments as suggested in the UNIFY rule UN 2.4 "Unify comments" and standardized comment references as suggested in UN 5.1 "Unify highlighting indicators" will help to understand comments better and faster.

SA 5   SUMMARIZE MESSAGE

Conclude a presentation with the overall message, including the next steps and an explanation of the consequences.

SA 5.1   REPEAT MESSAGE

Avoid the phrase "Thank you for your attention" at the end of a presentation. Instead, presenters should briefly sum up their message one last time – in one sentence, if possible. At the conclusion of a successful presentation, the audience will be thanking the presenters for the information. Repeating the message from the beginning of a presentation at the end helps the audience check the quality of the storyline and brings the presentation full circle. In reports, on the other hand, such repetition is not necessary as the reader can quickly browse back to the respective summary at the beginning.

Figure SA 5.1: Repeat message

SA 5.2 EXPLAIN CONSEQUENCES

Conclude reports and presentations with proposals for decisions to be taken and an explanation of their consequences. This is the real objective of a presentation: Convince the audience of both the message and the suggested steps to be taken next.

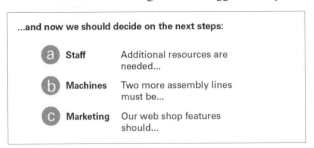

Figure SA 5.2: Explain consequences

STRUCTURE – ORGANIZE CONTENT

STRUCTURE covers all aspects of organizing the content of reports, presentations, and dashboards. *Organizing the content* means that they follow a logical structure forming a convincing storyline.

This chapter covers using consistent elements, building non-overlapping elements, building collectively exhaustive elements, building hierarchical structures, and visualizing their structure properly.

ST 1   USE CONSISTENT ELEMENTS

Listings and groupings of any kind of elements (items, terms, pictures, symbols, etc.) used to organize content in charts, tables, and texts should contain consistent elements only. This pertains for example to items, statements, wordings, and the appearance of symbols and pictures.

ST 1.1   USE CONSISTENT ITEMS

Items in a group should be of the same type, i.e. consistent. Consistent items can be different types of cars, houses, traffic signs, or – as shown in Figure ST 1.1, on the right hand side – different national flags representing the corresponding nations. The left hand side of this figure includes other types of items besides national flags, destroying the consistency.

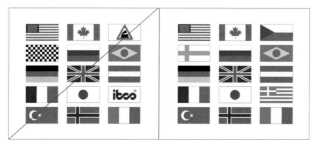

Figure ST 1.1: Use consistent items

ST 1.2   USE CONSISTENT TYPES OF STATEMENTS

A list of statements will be easier to understand if all statements are of the same type. The right hand side of Figure ST 1.2 shows four suggestions. By contrast, on the left-hand side of this figure the third statement is a detection, not a suggestion.

Figure ST 1.2: Use consistent types of statements

ST 1.3 USE CONSISTENT WORDING

Structure all phrases – especially in listed arrangements – in a grammatically consistent manner to facilitate quicker understanding. The right hand side of Figure ST 1.3 shows a group of four consistent suggestions, an imperative verb paired with a noun. By contrast, on the left hand side of this figure the second suggestion uses verbal substantive instead of an imperative.

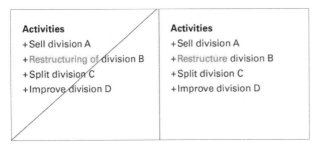

Figure ST 1.3: Use consistent wording

ST 1.4 USE CONSISTENT VISUALIZATIONS

Visualizations such as symbols and pictures that are uniform in respect to their layouts, colors, forms, fonts, etc. – especially in listed arrangements – facilitate faster and easier comprehension.

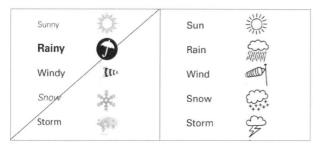

Figure ST 1.4: Use consistent visualizations

Ultimately, this rule describes how the consistent notation of structural dimensions as suggested in the UNIFY rule UN 3.4 "Unify structure dimensions" helps to perceive them more quickly.

ST 2 BUILD NON-OVERLAPPING ELEMENTS

Elements belonging to a group should not overlap, i.e. they should be mutually exclusive. This concerns practical applications such as report structures, business measures, or structure dimensions.

ST 2.1 BUILD NON-OVERLAPPING REPORT STRUCTURES

Structure reports and presentations in such a way that the parts, chapters, sections, and paragraphs do not overlap. They should not cover the same aspects.

In Figure ST 2.1, on the left hand side, the following chapters of a project description overlap:

- expenses and costs
- schedule, steps, milestones, and calendar
- objective, results, and achievements

At first glance, the six terms on the right hand side of this figure have no overlap in their logical structure. Of course, a relationship exists between the *cost*, the *results*, and the *schedule* of a project, but in regards to the content of the chapters this is not an overlap.

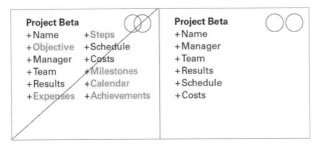

Figure ST 2.1: Build non-overlapping report structures

ST 2.2 BUILD NON-OVERLAPPING BUSINESS MEASURES

Structure a group of business measures in lists or calculations in a way they do not overlap, i.e. business measures on one hierarchical level should be disjoint or mutually exclusive.

Looking at Figure ST 2.2, on the left hand side, the following business measures overlap

- *material costs* and *costs of goods sold*
- *depreciation* and *fixed costs*

The calculation scheme on the right hand side has been cleaned up.

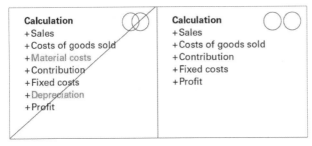

Figure ST 2.2: Build non-overlapping business measures

ST 2.3 BUILD NON-OVERLAPPING STRUCTURE DIMENSIONS

The elements of the structure dimensions used in reports and presentations should not overlap, i.e. the elements of a structure dimension should be disjoint or mutually exclusive.

Looking at Figure ST 2.3 on the left hand side, the regions *Norway, Sweden, Denmark,* and *Finland* overlap with *Scandinavia.*

Figure ST 2.3: Build non-overlapping structure dimensions

ST 3   BUILD COLLECTIVELY EXHAUSTIVE ELEMENTS

A list of elements is considered to be exhaustive when they cover all aspects of a superordinate topic. For example, dividing *Europe* into *Germany*, *Austria*, *Switzerland*, and *Belgium* is not exhaustive because other countries also belong to Europe.

Structures with mutually exclusive (ME) and collectively exhaustive (CE) elements are known as MECE structures.

ST 3.1   BUILD EXHAUSTIVE ARGUMENTS

If some important arguments relating to a specific question are left out, the given answer will not be convincing.

Looking at Figure ST 3.1 on the left hand side the option "*old products, new location*" is missing.

Figure ST 3.1: Build exhaustive arguments

ST 3.2   BUILD EXHAUSTIVE STRUCTURES

The elements of structures presented e.g. in charts and tables should also be exhaustive, in other words, adding up to one hundred percent.

In many practical applications of this kind, adding a remainder element ("rest of...") helps to conform to this rule.

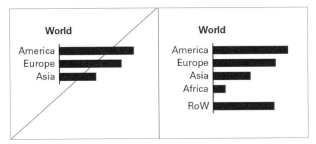

Figure ST 3.2: Build exhaustive structures in charts and tables

A consistent notation of remainder elements in charts and tables will help to perceive the exhaustiveness of a structure instantly (see EXPRESS rules EX 1.1 "Use appropriate chart types" and EX 1.2 "Use appropriate table types").

ST 4   BUILD HIERARCHICAL STRUCTURES

Give reports and presentations a hierarchical structure whenever possible, resulting in faster comprehension and simplified searching. These rules help to write and present a good storyline.

ST 4.1   USE DEDUCTIVE REASONING

Exhibiting deductive reasoning (*logical flow*) for a given message aids in building hierarchical structures. *Logical flows* always answer the question "why" following the key message. They begin with a statement (all men are mortal), continue with a comment (Socrates is a man), and resolve with a conclusion (Socrates is mortal) culminating in the message (Socrates will die).

Deductive reasoning can be best applied in controversial discussions for arguing and demonstrating need for action. However, it forces the readers or the audience to reproduce the deduction and the whole argumentation can collapse if any statements are questionable.

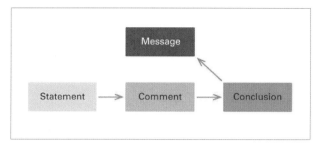

Figure ST 4.1: Use deductive reasoning

ST 4.2 USE INDUCTIVE REASONING

Exhibiting *inductive* reasoning (*logical group*) for a given message aids in understanding hierarchical structures. *Logical groups* are homogenous, non-overlapping, and collectively exhaustive arguments culminating in a message. This results in a powerful argumentation that satisfies the addressees need for an easily comprehensible logical structure.

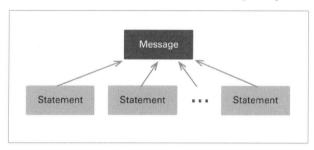

Figure ST 4.2: Use inductive reasoning

ST 5 VISUALIZE STRUCTURE

Having organized the arguments hierarchically, visualize this structure in order to make the storyline transparent.

ST 5.1 VISUALIZE STRUCTURE IN REPORTS

For easier understanding, underscore the logical structure of reports and presentations with visual aids (e.g. outlines, dashboards, summaries). Figure ST 5.1 illustrates this rule showing binder tabs on the right hand side.

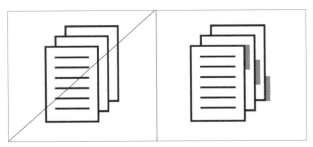

Figure ST 5.1: Visualize structure in reports

ST 5.2 VISUALIZE STRUCTURE IN TABLES

Design tables in such a manner that their structure can be recognized in both the columns as well as the rows.

The right hand side of Figure ST 5.2 shows three hierarchical levels of rows in a table. The base level shows cities, the first summary shows regions, and the second summary shows the country.

	J	F	M	Q1		J	F	M	Q1
Hamburg	12	11	9	32	Hamburg	12	11	9	32
Berlin	19	16	14	49	Berlin	19	16	14	49
North	31	27	23	81	**North**	**31**	**27**	**23**	**81**
Munich	16	14	15	45	Munich	16	14	15	45
Stuttgart	23	20	21	64	Stuttgart	23	20	21	64
South	39	34	36	109	**South**	**39**	**34**	**36**	**109**
Germany	70	61	59	190	**Germany**	**70**	**61**	**59**	**190**

Figure ST 5.2: Visualize structure in tables

The consistent semantic notation of row and column types in tables as suggested in the EXPRESS rule EX 1.2 "Use appropriate table types" will accelerate the perception of structures in tables.

ST 5.3 VISUALIZE STRUCTURE IN NOTES

Notes are also easier to understand when their structure is shown clearly (see Figure ST 5.3).

Figure ST 5.3: Visualize structure in notes

A consistent design of comments as suggested in the UNIFY rule UN 2.4 "Unify comments" and standardized comment references as suggested in UN 5.1 "Unify highlighting indicators" will support comprehension of structures in notes.

PERCEPTUAL RULES

The *perceptual rules* from the EXPRESS, CHECK, CONDENSE, and SIMPLIFY sections of the SUCCESS formula help to clearly relay content by using an appropriate visual design. They are based on the work of authors such as William Playfair[10], Willard Cope Brinton[11], Gene Zelazny[12], Edward Tufte[13], and Stephen Few[14].

---

[10] Playfair, William: The Commercial and Political Atlas, 1786
[11] Brinton, Willard Cope: Graphic Methods For Presenting Facts, 1914
[12] Zelazny, Gene: Say it with charts, 4th edition, 2001
[13] Tufte, Edward: The Visual Display of Quantitative Information, 2nd edition, 2011
[14] Few, Stephen: Show Me the Numbers, 2nd edition, 2012

EXPRESS – CHOOSE PROPER VISUALIZATION

EXPRESS covers all aspects of choosing the proper visualization in reports, presentations and dashboards.

Proper visualization means that charts and tables help easily identify interesting facts in *statistics* and quickly convey the desired message in *reports*.

This chapter covers utilizing the correct types of charts and tables, replacing inappropriate visualizations and representations, adding comparisons, and explaining causes.

EX 1   USE APPROPRIATE OBJECT TYPES

Choosing the appropriate *object type* is of prime importance for the comprehension of reports, presentations, and dashboards.

We use tables when looking up data. Tables have a high information density. They are clear, they are honest, they do not want to highlight, and they typically do not want to visually convey a certain message. So they do not compete with charts.

Charts on the opposite are always biased, especially when they are used to convey a message. It is the selection of data, the selection of the chart type, and the usage of highlighting which makes the difference. We evaluate charts by asking whether they transfer the intended message effectively and in a proper way. So charts in reports conveying messages cannot be replaced by tables.

The following section is about choosing the appropriate types of charts and tables. It presents in detail different types, layouts, and examples as well as their proper application.

EX 1.1   USE APPROPRIATE CHART TYPES

A *chart* is a graphical object, in which visualization elements such as columns, bars, and lines represent data.

This section discusses the types, layout, and examples of *single charts*. *Overlay charts* and *multiple charts* are discussed in the CONDENSE rules CO 4 "Add elements" and CO 5 "Add objects".

The most important groups of business charts are those showing development over time (charts with horizontal category axes), those showing structural relationships (charts with vertical category axes), and those showing x-y charts, scatter plots, and bubble charts (charts with two value axes), see Figure EX 1.1.

Other chart types are of lesser interest in business communication and will be treated in a later version of the standards.

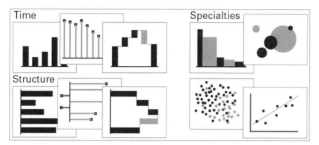

Figure EX 1.1: Use appropriate chart types

Looking at charts with horizontal and vertical category axes, the chart selection matrix displayed in Figure EX 1.1-1 aids in selecting the right chart type for time series and structure analyses.

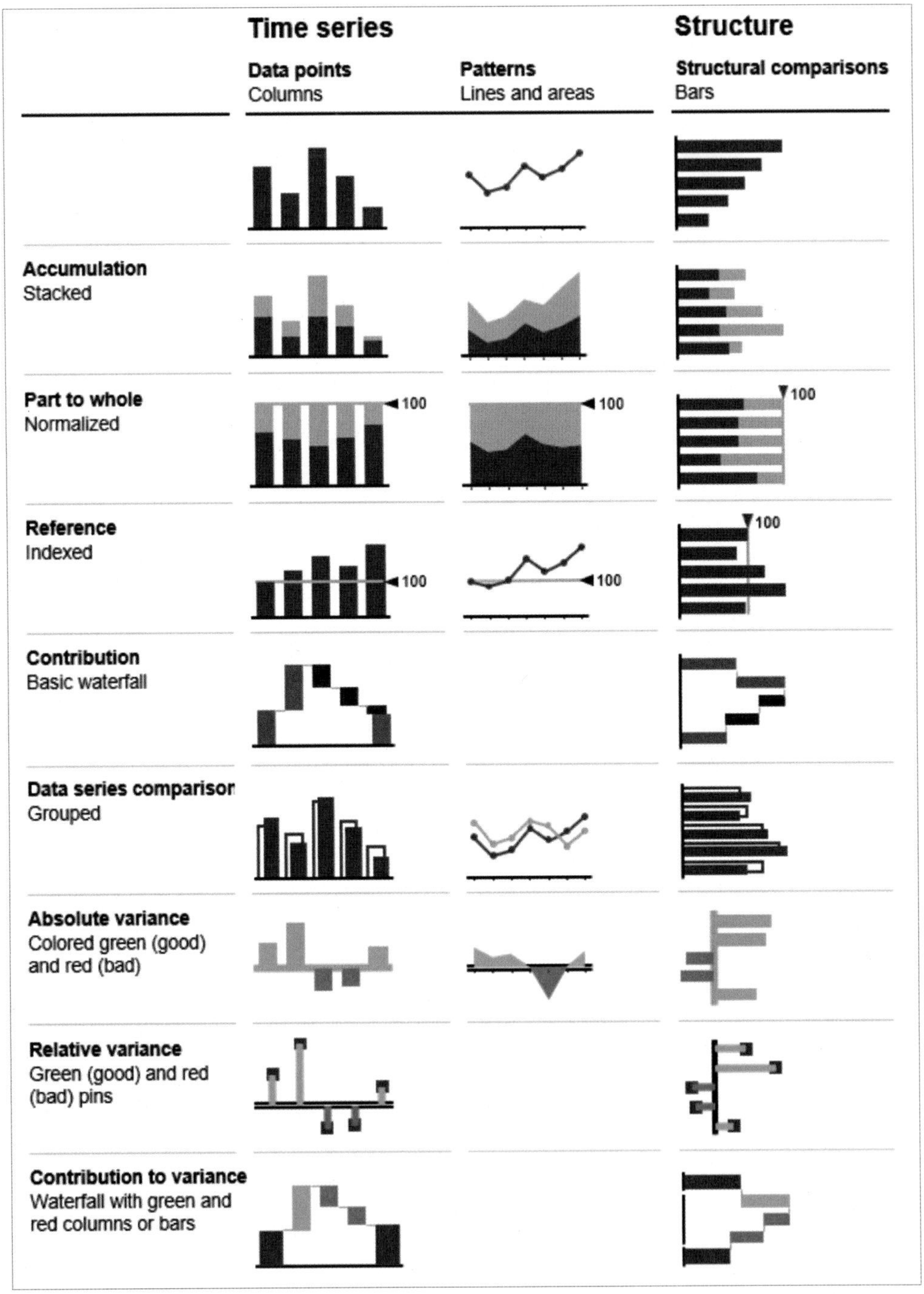
Time series
Structure
Data points
Columns
Patterns
Lines and areas
Structural comparisons
Bars
Accumulation
Stacked
Part to whole
Normalized
100
100
100
Reference
Indexed
100
100
100
Contribution
Basic waterfall
Data series comparison
Grouped
Absolute variance
Colored green (good)
and red (bad)
Relative variance
Green (good) and red
(bad) pins
Contribution to variance
Waterfall with green and
red columns or bars

Figure EX 1.1-1: Chart types for time series and structure analyses (conceptual)

In the following sections, the correct usage of charts with *horizontal* category axes, charts with *vertical* category axes, and charts with *two* value axes is discussed in greater detail.

CHARTS WITH HORIZONTAL CATEGORY AXES

According to UNIFY rule UN 3.3 "Unify time periods and points in time", charts with horizontal category axes (short: *horizontal charts*) typically display time series. Use the horizontal category axis as a time axis. Vertically, the visualization elements represent the data per time period or point of time (there is no need to show a vertical value axis as the visualization elements carry their own values). Time category axes run from left to right and show characteristics of period types (e.g. months or years) or points of time (dates).

In general, the data series of a *horizontal chart* is represented by columns (single, stacked, grouped), vertical pins, horizontal waterfalls, or lines. *Vertical pins* can be considered very thin columns. Because of their importance for the IBCS, they are dealt with in a separate section.

Here follows the grouping of *horizontal chart types*:

Single column charts

In general, *single column charts* (short: single columns) are used to display the temporal evolvement of one data series, see Figure EX 1.1-2.

Single columns consist of:

- **Horizontal category axis:** The *horizontal category axis* represents with its labels the respective time periods or points of time. UNIFY rule UN 3.3 "Unify time periods" suggests to use the category width for identifying the period type if helpful (see width A in Figure EX 1.1-2).
- **Columns**: One *column* per time period or point of time extends from the category axis in accordance with the respective value. Columns are displayed in the foreground of the category axis, so that the length of the column is not hidden. According to UNIFY rule UN 3.1 "Unify measures" the ratio of column width to category width (see ratio B/A in Figure EX 1.1-2) represents information about the measure type (basic measure vs ratio).
- **Legends**: As there is only one data series, the legend (name of the data series) is part of the chart title.
- **Data labels**: *Data labels* name the values of the data series corresponding to the length of the respective columns. According to UNIFY rule UN 2.3 "Unify the position of legends and labels", columns with positive values (pointing upward) are labeled above, columns with negative values (pointing downward) below the column.

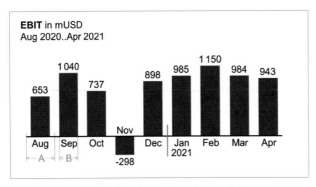

Figure EX 1.1-2: Single column chart (example)

Stacked column charts

Stacked column charts (short: stacked columns) represent more than one data series (e.g. multiple products, countries, or divisions), see Figure EX 1.1-3.

Stacked columns consist of:

- **Horizontal category axis:** See single column charts.
- **Columns**: The columns (see single column charts) are divided into segments (Excel names them "data points") representing the data series (stacked columns).
- **Legends**: According to UNIFY rule UN 2.3 "Unify the position of legends and labels", legends (names of the data series) are positioned either on the far left side with right-aligned text or on the far right side with left-aligned text. They are vertically centered within the corresponding column segments. If a segment at the far left or far right is missing or has a very small size, its legends might need assisting lines.
- **Data labels**: *Data labels* name the values of the data series corresponding to the length of the respective column segments. According to UNIFY rule UN 2.3 "Unify the position of legends and labels" the labels of the segments are positioned within the segments. If the sum of the column segments of a category is positive (column pointing upward), the label of the sum is positioned above the respective column, if negative (column pointing downward), it is positioned below.

It must be pointed out that stacked columns should only be used if all chart values are either positive or negative.

This chart type might also not be a good choice if the values of each data series vary too much. The maximum number of data series (segments of a stacked column) to be shown depends on the range of how much the values of each data series vary: More than 5 data series will only work well in the case of little variations.

Position the data series of central importance or interest directly on the axis in order to best see its development over time.

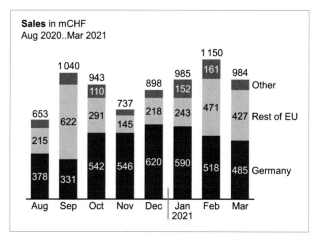

Figure EX 1.1-3: Stacked column chart (example)

Grouped column charts

Grouped column charts (short: grouped columns) show, in general, time series for a primary scenario (e.g. AC or FC) in comparison with a reference scenario (e.g. PY or PL). Two columns per category (*grouped columns*) represent these two scenarios.

The columns of the primary scenario and the reference scenario overlap, the reference scenario placed behind the primary scenario (see bottom chart of Figure EX 1.1-4) – either to the left or right of the primary scenario depending on the creation date of the scenario as defined in the paragraph on "Scenario comparisons" in the UNIFY rule UN 4.1 "Unify scenario analyses". A third scenario could be displayed using a *reference scenario triangle*. All other elements of a grouped column chart are identical to single column charts.

Instead of using grouped columns, the primary scenario can be represented with a single column with the reference scenario represented by reference scenario triangles (see top chart of Figure EX 1.1-4).

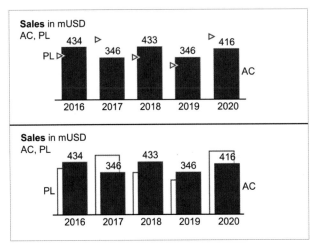

Figure EX 1.1-4: Grouped column chart and reference scenario triangles (examples)

Horizontal pin charts

According to UNIFY rule UN 4.1 "Unify scenario analyses", *horizontal pin charts* (short: horizontal pins) are used for the visualization of relative variances in a time series analysis, see Figure EX 1.1-5.

Horizontal pins consist of:

- **Horizontal category axis:** see *single column chart*.
- **Pins**: One *pin* per time period or point of time extends from the category axis to the respective length. The pin has the size of a very thin column. Color the pin green or red corresponding with positive or negative relative variances respectively. The fill of the pinhead represents the primary scenario (see the paragraph on "Scenario comparisons" in the UNIFY rule UN 4.1 "Unify scenario analyses"). Display the pin in the foreground, so that the length of the pin (see length X in Figure EX 1.1-5) is not hidden.
- **Legends**: As there is only one data series, the legend (name of the data series) is part of the chart title.
- **Data labels**: *Data labels* name the values of the data series consistent with the length of the respective pins. Position the labels of positive values above the respective pins, labels of negative values below (UNIFY rule UN 2.3 "Unify the position of legends and labels").

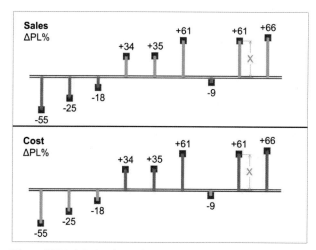

Figure EX 1.1-5: Horizontal pin chart showing relative variances (example)

Horizontal waterfall charts

Horizontal waterfall charts (short: *horizontal waterfalls* or *column waterfalls*) analyze root causes, over time, for the change or variance between two or more statuses. Accordingly, horizontal waterfalls consist of two or more *base columns* and *totals columns*. In between a base column and a totals column there are *contribution columns* demonstrating what led to the difference between these two columns. The *contribution columns* start at the end value, i.e. the height, of the preceding column, and show the positive or negative contribution as well as the accumulated contribution of all columns up to the respective point of time.

There are two types of horizontal waterfalls:

Growth waterfalls: In *growth waterfalls*, base columns and totals columns represent a stock measure (e.g. headcount, accounts receivable) at different points in time (e.g. end of 2018, 2019 and 2020), see Figure EX 1.1-6. The contribution columns in between represent the changes (increases and decreases) over time of this stock measure.

(There is no vertical equivalent to the horizontal *growth waterfall*.)

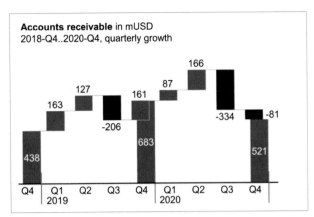

Figure EX 1.1-6: Growth waterfall (example)

Horizontal variance waterfalls: In *horizontal variance waterfalls*, base columns and totals columns represent a flow measure (e.g. sales) at different periods in time (e.g. 2019 and 2020) and/or regarding different scenarios (e.g. PL and AC). The contribution columns in between represent the periodical variances between the different time periods and/or scenarios, see Figure EX 1.1-7.

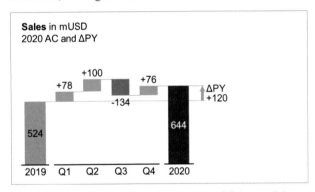

Figure EX 1.1-7: Horizontal variance waterfall (example)

The elements of a horizontal waterfall chart are the same as the elements of single column charts. In addition, *assisting lines* connect the end of a column to the beginning of the succeeding column.

Line charts

In general, *line charts* are used for the display of the temporal evolvement of data series with many data points, see Figure EX 1.1-8 and Figure EX 1.1-9.

Many data points lead to small category widths. The advantage of line charts over column charts is the simplified display of data (better *data-ink-ratio*[15]). In addition, they can better represent positive and negative values of more than one data series than columns. On the other hand, lines tend to imply a continuous timeline – practically non-existent in business communication. Therefore lines should not be used for the presentation of data series with only a few values.

Line charts cannot be "stacked" in order to show structure like in stacked column charts. In the place of line charts for "stacked data", *area charts* offer a good solution (there is no layout concept for area charts in this version of IBCS yet).

Line charts with more than three intersecting lines tend to be confusing. Instead, several smaller charts with one line each could be placed next to one another (small multiples), particularly when the general trends of the lines are to be analyzed – not the direct comparison of two data series (e.g. in comparing seasonal developments of several years), see also EX 2.4 "Replace spaghetti charts".

Line charts consist of:

- **Horizontal category axis:** See *single column chart*. The UNIFY rule UN 3.3 "Unify time periods" suggests to use the category width (see width A in Figure EX 1.1-8) for identifying the period if helpful.
- **Lines**: One or more *lines* with *line markers* represent the values of the respective data series. Use line thickness, line color, and line markers for meaning, see part "Semantic rules".
- **Legends**: *Legends* label the data series. If the line chart shows only one data series, include the legend in the chart title. If the line chart shows two or more data series, the legend should be positioned to the right of the far right data point (left-aligned text, see Figure EX 1.1-8) or the left of the far left data point (right-aligned text, see Figure EX 1.1-9). Alternatively position legends close to the lines at any other place in the chart.
- **Data labels**: *Data labels* name the values of the respective data points. If possible, label maximum values (peaks) above the line markers and minimum values (valleys) below the line markers. In many practical applications it is not necessary to clutter the line

---

[15] The data-ink ratio is defined as the proportion of graphic's ink devoted to the non-redundant display of data-information, see Tufte, Edward: The Visual Display of Quantitative Information", 2nd edition, March 2011, page 93

chart by labeling every data point, see Figure EX 1.1-9 and the SIMPLIFY rule SI 5.3 "Avoid unnecessary labels".

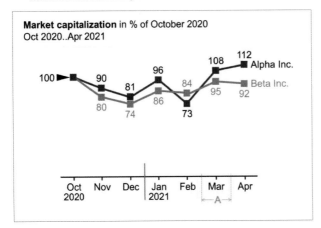

Figure EX 1.1-8: Line chart (example)

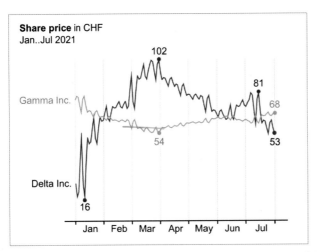

Figure EX 1.1-9: Line chart with selective data labels (example)

Other horizontal charts

Other chart types with horizontal category axes are *boxplot charts* (range charts) and *area charts*. There is no specific notation concept for these chart types yet however it can be easily derived from the notation concept of column and line charts.

CHARTS WITH VERTICAL CATEGORY AXES

According to UNIFY rule UN 3.4 "Unify structure dimensions, use vertical axes", charts with vertical category axes (*vertical charts*) typically show structural data. In general, present structural data of one period or one point of time in the form of *bars*.

Use the vertical category as a structure axis. Horizontally, the visualization elements represent the data per structure element (there is no need for a horizontal value axis as the visualization elements carry their own values). Structure axes run from top to bottom and show characteristics of structures (e.g. products or countries). The sequence of these elements depends on the intended analysis; see the UNIFY section about "Structure analyses".

In general, the data series of a vertical chart is represented by (horizontal) *bars* (single, stacked, grouped), by *horizontal pins*, or by *waterfall bars*. Do not use lines in vertical charts as they could be interpreted as trends or developments, which do not exist in structure analyses.

Horizontal pins can be considered very thin bars, but because of their importance for IBCS are dealt with in a separate section. A chart with horizontal pins is called a *vertical pin chart*.

Here follows the grouping of *vertical chart types*:

Single bar charts

In general, *single bar charts* (short: single bars) are used for the structural analysis of one data series (e.g., products, countries, or divisions) for one period or one point in time, see Figure EX 1.1-10.

Single bar charts consist of:

- **Vertical category axis:** The *vertical category axis* with its labels represents the respective structure elements such as countries, products, etc. The category width (see width A in Figure EX 1.1-10) should be the same for corresponding analyses.
- **Bars**: One *bar* per structure element extends from the category axis to the length representing the respective value. Display the bars in the foreground of the category axis, so that the length of the bar is not hidden. The IBCS part on "Semantic rules" suggests that the ratio of bar width to category width (see ratio B/A in Figure EX 1.1-10) represents information about the measure type (see the UNIFY rule UN 3.1 "Unify measures").
- **Legends**: As there is only one data series, the legend (name of the data series) is part of the chart title.
- **Data labels**: *Data labels* name the values of the data series consistent with the length of the respective bars. According to UNIFY rule UN 2.3 "Unify the position of legends

and labels" the labels of positive values are positioned at the right hand side of the respective bars, the labels of negative values at the left hand side.

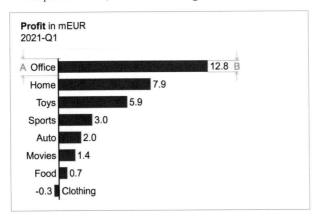

Figure EX 1.1-10: Single bar chart (example)

Stacked bar charts

Stacked bar charts (short: stacked bars) represent more than one data series (e.g., products, countries, or divisions) for one period or one point in time, see Figure EX 1.1-11.

Stacked bar charts consist of:

- **Vertical category axis**: See single bar charts.
- **Bars**: The bars (see single bar charts) are divided into segments (Excel names them "data points") representing the data series (stacked bars).
- **Legends**: Legends (names of the data series) are positioned either above the top stacked bar or below the bottom stacked bar and horizontally centered within the corresponding bar segments. If a segment at the top or bottom is missing or has a very small size, its legend might need assisting lines.
- **Data labels**: *Data labels* name the values of the data series corresponding to the length of the respective bar segment. If the sum of the bar segments of a category is positive (bar pointing to the right), the label of the sum is positioned to the right hand side of the respective bar. If the sum is negative (bar pointing to the left), the label of the sum is positioned to the left hand side of the respective bar.

It must be pointed out that stacked bars should only be used if all chart values are either positive or negative.

This chart type might also not be a good choice if the values of each data series vary too much. The maximum number of data series (segments of a stacked bars) to be shown depends on the range of how much the values of each data series vary: More than 5 data series will only work well in the case of little variations.

Position the data series of central interest directly at the axis in order to best see its structure.

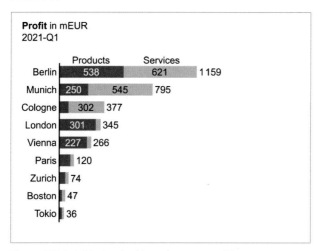

Profit in mEUR
2021-Q1

Figure EX 1.1-11: Stacked bar chart (example)

Grouped bar charts

In general, *grouped bar charts* (short: grouped bars) show structure analyses for a primary scenario (e.g. AC or FC) in comparison to a reference scenario (e.g. PY or PL). Two bars per category (*grouped bars)* represent *these* two scenarios.

The bars of the primary scenario and the reference scenario overlap, the reference scenario placed behind the primary scenario (see the bottom chart of Figure EX 1.1-12) – either above or below depending on the creation date of the scenario as defined in the paragraph on "Scenario comparisons" in the UNIFY rule UN 4.1 "Unify scenario analyses").

A third scenario could be displayed using a *reference scenario triangle*. All other elements of a grouped bar chart are identical to a single bar chart.

Alternatively, instead of grouped bars, the primary scenario can be represented with a single bar and the reference scenario by reference scenario triangles (see top chart of Figure EX 1.1-12).

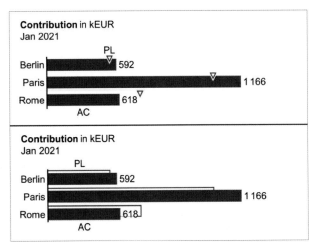

Figure EX 1.1-12: Grouped bar charts and reference scenario triangles (examples)

Vertical pin charts

Vertical pin charts (short: vertical pins) are used for the visualization of relative variances in a structure analysis, see Figure EX 1.1-13.

Vertical pins consist of:

- **Vertical category axis**: see *single bar chart*.
- **Pins**: One *pin* per structure element extends from the category axis to the respective length. The pin has the size of a very thin bar. It is colored green or red when representing positive or negative relative variances respectively. The fill of the pinhead represents the primary scenario (see the paragraph on "Scenario comparisons" in the UNIFY rule UN 4.1 "Unify scenario analyses"). Display pins in the foreground, so that the length of the pin (see length X in Figure EX 1.1-13) is not hidden.
- **Legends**: As there is only one data series, the legend (name of the data series) is part of the chart title.
- **Data labels**: *Data labels* name the values of the data series corresponding to the length of the respective pins. Position the labels of positive values at the right hand side of the respective pins, the labels of negative values at the left hand side.

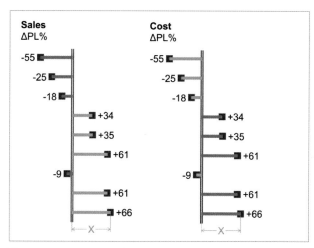

Figure EX 1.1-13: Vertical pin chart (example)

Vertical waterfall charts

Vertical waterfalls charts (in short: *vertical waterfalls* or *bar waterfalls*) analyze structural root causes for the difference between two or more statuses. Accordingly, vertical waterfalls consist of two or more *base bars* and *totals bars*. In between a base bar and a totals bar there are *contribution bars* representing the contribution to the difference between these two bars. Starting from the top base bar, *contribution bars* always start at the end of the preceding bar, showing positive or negative individual contributions of the respective structure element as well as the accumulated contribution resulting in the next totals bar.

There are two types of vertical waterfalls:

Calculation waterfalls: In *calculation waterfalls*, base bars and totals bars represent base and result measures (e.g. sales and EBIT) whereas the contribution bars in between represent the additions and subtractions of other measures (e.g. financial income and direct cost) in a calculation scheme. More complex calculation schemes (e.g. profit and loss calculation) can have intermediate subtotals bars, see Figure EX 1.1-14.

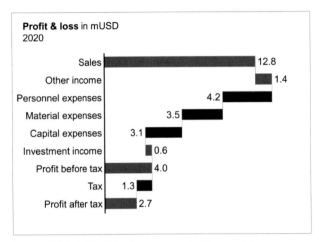

Figure EX 1.1-14: Calculation waterfall (example)

(There is no horizontal correspondence to the vertical *calculation waterfall*.)

Vertical variance waterfalls: In *vertical variance waterfalls*, base bars and totals bars represent values at different periods or points in time (e.g. Jan 2020 and Jan 2021) and/or different scenarios (e.g. PY and AC). The contribution bars in between represent the variances in structure between the different times and/or scenarios, see Figure EX 1.1-15.

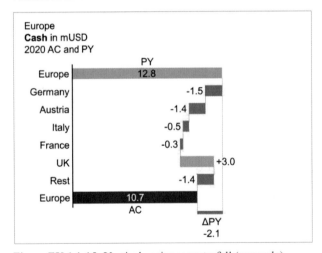

Figure EX 1.1-15: Vertical variance waterfall (example)

The elements of vertical waterfalls are the same as the elements of single bar charts. In addition, *assisting lines* connect the end of a bar with the beginning of the succeeding bar.

Remainder bar

If a large number of elements need to be presented, then only the most important elements can be displayed in one chart or on one page. In order to make the analyses exhaustive, sort the elements by descending size, accumulating the smallest elements, which cannot be depicted, in a *remainder bar* ("rest of..."), see Figure EX 1.1-16. Separate the remainder bar from the other bars by a wider gap (see gap C in Figure EX 1.1-16).

Note: This remainder bar has to be excluded from some structure analyses such as averaging, ranking, and selecting.

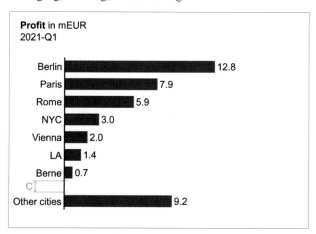

Figure EX 1.1-16: Single bar chart showing a remainder bar at the bottom (example)

Other vertical charts

Other chart types with vertical category axes are *vertical boxplot charts* (range charts). There is no specific notation concept for this chart type yet however it can be derived from the notation of the standard bar charts.

In general, do not use lines and areas in vertical charts as they might underline a continuum of data non-existent in business communication.

CHARTS WITH TWO VALUE AXES

Charts with two value axes show two-dimensional positioning of visualization elements, which can provide new and interesting insights. *Scattergrams* arrange points in a two-dimensional coordinate system, see Figure EX 1.1-17.

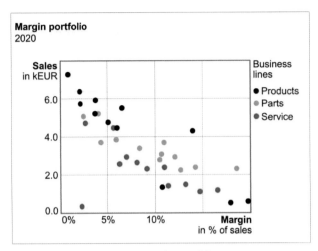

Figure EX 1.1-17: Scattergram (example)

Bubble charts (portfolio charts) have bubbles instead of points and use the bubble area to show a third dimension, see Figure EX 1.1-18. A fourth dimension could be presented via pie segments within the bubbles (bubble pie charts).

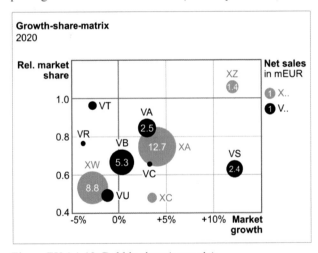

Figure EX 1.1-18: Bubble chart (example)

Besides *scattergrams* and *bubble charts* there are other chart types with two value axes, e.g. charts with horizontal axes representing a continuous timeline (instead of fixed time categories) and charts with columns or bars of variable width.

There are no specific notation rules for charts with two value axes yet. An appropriate notation concept for these chart types can be derived from the notation of column charts, bar charts and line charts with their data visualization elements, legends, data labels, and axes.

EX 1.2 USE APPROPRIATE TABLE TYPES

A *table* is a communication object in which data is arranged in two dimensions, i.e. (vertical) *columns and* (horizontal) *rows*. The *row header* (row name) describes the content of a row, the *column header* (column name) the content of a column. The data are positioned at the intersections of rows and columns called *table cells*.

"One-dimensional tables" (tables with one or more columns but without row headers) are called *lists* and are not covered here.

Table types are defined by a set of *columns* and a set of *rows* in order to fulfill specific analytic and/or reporting purposes. The following definitions for columns and rows cover both their content and their semantic design for visual recognition of the content. They may therefore be considered complementary to the semantic notation rules described in the UNIFY chapter.

COLUMN TYPES

Column types are columns with similar content falling under similar column headers. Typical column types are *time columns* (with monthly or yearly data), *scenario columns* (with actual or plan data) and *variance columns* (ΔPL or ΔPY).

The following layout principles apply to all column types:

- **Width**: Columns belonging to a certain column type should have an identical width. This column width should not depend on the text length of the respective column header.
- **Orientation**: Right-align columns with numerical data. Left-align columns with non-numerical data (e.g. texts or product names). *Column headers* have the same orientation as the rest of the column. Headers for combined columns can be centered or even left-aligned to increase legibility.
- **Vertical lines and gaps**: Vertical lines separating different columns should be very light or even omitted. Use white vertical lines or white vertical gaps to mark the columns. In the following figures, different widths of these white lines resp. gaps are being used to separate and group columns. Separate columns of the same type by a narrow gap (see gap B1 in Figure EX 1.2-2 et seq.). Use a wider gap to separate a group of similar columns from the next group (see gap B2 in Figure EX 1.2-1 et seq.).

Additional layout principles depend on the *column types* described below.

Row header columns

Row header columns contain the header texts of the rows. Often, these columns are positioned at the very left of a table. In most cases, row header columns are much wider than other column types.

Keep the texts of the row headers short by using abbreviations or footnotes in order to omit too wide tables.

Use a wider gap (see width B2 in Figure EX 1.2-1) to separate the *row header column* from columns with numbers.

Electronic Inc.
Net sales in mEUR
2021-Q1

B2	PY	PL	AC	ΔPY	ΔPY%	ΔPL	ΔPL%
Austria	560	590	559	-1	-0%	-31	-5%
Belgium	56	72	58	+2	+4%	-14	-19%
France	140	149	134	-6	-4%	-15	-10%
Germany	345	279	260	-85	-25%	-19	-7%
Poland	78	91	86	+8	+10%	-5	-5%
Sweden	77	81	86	+9	+12%	+5	+6%
Italy	61	70	66	+5	+8%	-4	-6%
Other	502	498	545	+43	+9%	+47	+9%
Europe	1 819	1 830	1 794	-25	-1%	-36	-2%

Figure EX 1.2-1: Row header column (example)

Scenario columns

Scenario columns show data for scenarios (e.g. previous year, plan, actual). Use the same width for all scenario columns (depending on the number of digits).

For the sequence of scenario columns see the UNIFY rule UN 4.1 "Unify scenario analyses".

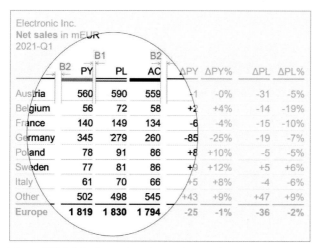

Electronic Inc.
Net sales in mEUR
2021-Q1

| | | B1 | B2 | | | | |
	B2 PY	PL	AC	ΔPY	ΔPY%	ΔPL	ΔPL%
Austria	560	590	559	-1	-0%	-31	-5%
Belgium	56	72	58	+2	+4%	-14	-19%
France	140	149	134	-6	-4%	-15	-10%
Germany	345	279	260	-85	-25%	-19	-7%
Poland	78	91	86	+8	+10%	-5	-5%
Sweden	77	81	86	+9	+12%	+5	+6%
Italy	61	70	66	+5	+8%	-4	-6%
Other	502	498	545	+43	+9%	+47	+9%
Europe	**1 819**	**1 830**	**1 794**	**-25**	**-1%**	**-36**	**-2%**

Figure EX 1.2-2: Scenario columns (example)

Variance columns

Variance columns show data of absolute variances (e.g. ΔPL, ΔPY) or relative variances (e.g. ΔPL%, ΔPY%).

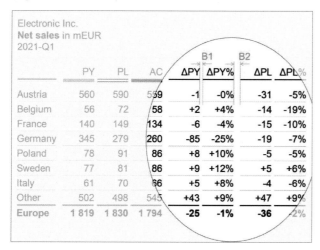

Electronic Inc.
Net sales in mEUR
2021-Q1

| | | | | B1 | B2 | | |
	PY	PL	AC	ΔPY	ΔPY%	ΔPL	ΔPL%
Austria	560	590	559	-1	-0%	-31	-5%
Belgium	56	72	58	+2	+4%	-14	-19%
France	140	149	134	-6	-4%	-15	-10%
Germany	345	279	260	-85	-25%	-19	-7%
Poland	78	91	86	+8	+10%	-5	-5%
Sweden	77	81	86	+9	+12%	+5	+6%
Italy	61	70	66	+5	+8%	-4	-6%
Other	502	498	545	+43	+9%	+47	+9%
Europe	**1 819**	**1 830**	**1 794**	**-25**	**-1%**	**-36**	**-2%**

Figure EX 1.2-3: Variance columns (example)

Time columns

Time columns show *time periods* (for flow measures) or *points of time* (for stock measures).

Follow UN 2.3 "Unify time periods and points of time" and use a temporal order - from left to right - for the sequence of the time columns (e.g. Jan, Feb, Mar, or 2019, 2020, 2021).

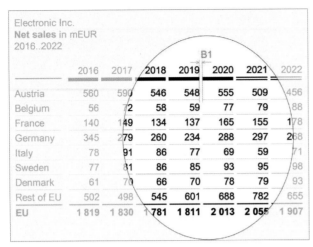

Electronic Inc.
Net sales in mEUR
2016..2022

	2016	2017	2018	2019	2020	2021	2022
Austria	560	590	**546**	**548**	**555**	**509**	456
Belgium	56	72	**58**	**59**	**77**	**79**	88
France	140	149	**134**	**137**	**165**	**155**	178
Germany	345	279	**260**	**234**	**288**	**297**	268
Italy	78	91	**86**	**77**	**69**	**59**	71
Sweden	77	81	**86**	**85**	**93**	**95**	98
Denmark	61	70	**66**	**70**	**78**	**79**	93
Rest of EU	502	498	**545**	**601**	**688**	**782**	655
EU	1 819	1 830	**1 781**	**1 811**	**2 013**	**2 055**	1 907

Figure EX 1.2-4: Time columns (example)

Measure columns

Measure columns show measures such as sales, headcount, or equity.

Displaying long measure names in column headers can be challenging. As the column width should not depend on the length of the measure name, use the abbreviations defined in the glossary instead.

Use a wider gap after intermediate results to expose the calculation scheme (see width B2 in Figure EX 1.2-5).

Electronic Inc.
Gross profit calculation in kCHF
2021-Q1

	Gross sales	Dis- counts	**Net sales**	Direct cost	**Contr. marg.**	Indirect costs	Gross profit
Austria	3 217	213	**3 004**	1 532	**1 472**	1 009	463
Belgium	245	72	**173**	46	**127**	77	50
France	3 467	288	**3 179**	1 109	**2 070**	1 674	396
Italy	8 754	788	**7 966**	4 478	**3 488**	3 055	433
Poland	3 411	455	**2 956**	1 230	**1 726**	1 105	621
Sweden	1 987	678	**1 309**	990	**319**	341	-22
Poland	499	111	**388**	231	**157**	118	39
Other	8 765	1 255	**7 510**	6 799	**711**	321	390
Europe	30 345	3 860	26 485	**16 415**	**10 070**	7 700	2 370

Figure EX 1.2-5: Measure columns (example)

Structure columns

Structure columns show the elements of a structure dimension (e.g. countries or products).

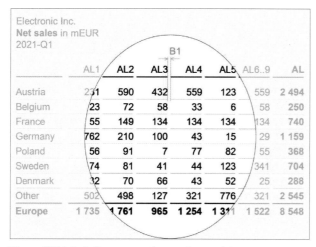

Electronic Inc. Net sales in mEUR 2021-Q1	AL1	AL2	AL3	B1 AL4	AL5	AL6..9	AL
Austria	231	590	432	559	123	559	2 494
Belgium	23	72	58	33	6	58	250
France	55	149	134	134	134	134	740
Germany	762	210	100	43	15	29	1 159
Poland	56	91	7	77	82	55	368
Sweden	74	81	41	44	123	341	704
Denmark	32	70	66	43	52	25	288
Other	502	498	127	321	776	321	2 545
Europe	1 735	1 761	965	1 254	1 311	1 522	8 548

Figure EX 1.2-6: Structure columns (example)

"Of which" columns

If details of an aggregated column are shown in one or more column not totaling to the aggregated column, these columns are called "of which" columns.

Use a consistent design for *of which columns* that differs from other columns. E.g. use a smaller font (see X in Figure EX 1.2-7) to expose an *of which column* and do not separate it from the mother column (see columns *AL3* and *AL3.1* in Figure EX 1.2-7) in order to show that it is part of it. An *of which column* is positioned at the right hand side of the mother column.

Electronic Inc.
Net sales in mEUR
2021-Q1

	AL1	AL2	AL3	of which AL3.1	AL4	AL5..9	AL
Austria	231	590	432	259	123	559	1 935
Belgium	23	72	58	33	6	58	217
France	55	149	134	26	134	134	606
Germany	762	210	100	43	15	29	1 116
Poland	56	91	7	2	82	55	291
Sweden	74	81	41	24	123	341	660
Denmark	32	70	66	29	52	25	245
Other	502	498	127	88	776	321	2 224
Europe	1 735	1 761	965	504	1 311	1 522	7 294

Figure EX 1.2-7: "Of which" column (example)

Remainder columns

If the set to be presented in the columns has too many elements, accumulate the less important or smaller elements in a *remainder* column (e.g. two columns for the two most important cost types and a remainder column titled "Other cost").

In Figure EX 1.2-8, the *remainder column* "Other cost" has the same vertical gaps B1 as the other measure columns.

Electronic Inc.
Gross profit calculation in kUSD
2021-Q1

	Net sales	Material cost	Staff cost	Other cost	Gross profit
Austria	3 217	1 322	1 345	325	225
Belgium	245	111	67	33	34
France	3 467	2 145	1 007	225	90
Germany	8 754	4 566	2 389	1 678	121
Poland	3 411	1 899	1 087	347	78
Sweden	1 987	1 210	789	121	-133
Switzerland	499	234	113	34	118
Other	8 765	4 509	2 347	561	1 348
Europe	30 345	15 996	9 144	3 324	1 881

Figure EX 1.2-8: Remainder column (example)

"Percent of" columns

Use *"Percent of"* columns to present important data of another column as shares of a given total. A typical example for a *"percent of"* column is data of a profit and loss statement as a percentage of sales, see Figure EX 1.2-9.

"Percent of" columns have a smaller font size (see X) than the other columns.

Electronic Inc.
Gross profit calculation in mUSD
2021

	Q1	Q2	Q3	Q4	**2021**	% of sales
Software	453	467	442	543	**1 905**	64,1
Support	87	99	123	132	**441**	(14,8)
Consulting	121	145	131	231	**628**	21,1
Sales	**661**	**711**	**696**	**906**	**2 974**	100,0
Cost of sales	231	282	285	199	**997**	33,5
Gross profit	**430**	**429**	**411**	**707**	**977**	66,5

Figure EX 1.2-9: "Percent of" column (example)

Totals columns

Position columns displaying *totals of a group of columns* (e.g. quarters totaling in years or products totaling in product groups) at the right hand side of the columns belonging to this group. The design of the *totals columns* should be consistent and different from other columns. The numbers are usually highlighted by bold fonts or the background can be filled e.g. by light gray if helpful.

Electronic Inc.
Gross profit calculation in kUSD
2021-Q1

	Net sales	Material cost	Staff cost	Other cost	**Gross profit**
Austria	3 217	1 322	1 345	325	**225**
Belgium	245	111	67	33	**34**
France	3 467	2 145	1 007	225	**90**
Germany	8 754	4 566	2 389	1 678	**121**
Poland	3 411	1 899	1 087	347	**78**
Sweden	1 987	1 210	789	121	**-133**
Switzerland	499	234	113	34	**118**
Other	8 765	4 509	2 347	561	**1 348**
Europe	**30 345**	**15 996**	**9 144**	**3 324**	**1 881**

Figure EX 1.2-10: Totals column (example)

The column types described before refer to *single* columns. The following paragraphs present *combined* columns i.e. *hierarchical* and *nested* columns.

Hierarchical columns

Hierarchies in dimensions may call for columns showing multiple levels. If possible, the sibling elements belonging to the same parent element of a dimension should be homogenous, mutually exclusive, and collectively exhaustive. The principles for structuring hierarchies are covered in the chapter "STRUCTURE - Organize content".

Separate parents by appropriate means, e.g. wider gaps. Display the parent columns at the right hand side of their child columns *(like totals columns)*.

In Figure EX 1.2-11, a wider gap B2 separates the two years (with four quarters each) from each other.

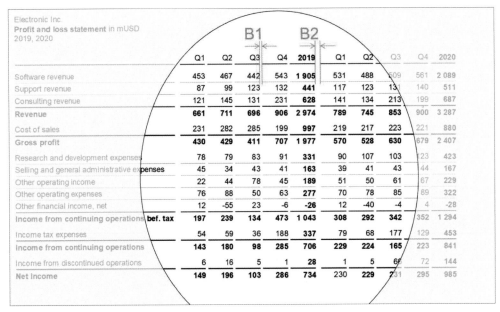

Figure EX 1.2-11: Hierarchical columns (example)

Nested columns

In *nested columns*, two column types are combined in such a way that the columns of one type repeat iteratively within every column of the other type. Separate the resulting groups of columns by appropriate means, e.g. wider gaps.

In Figure EX 1.2-12, wider gaps B2 separate the four years (with AC and PL data each) from each other.

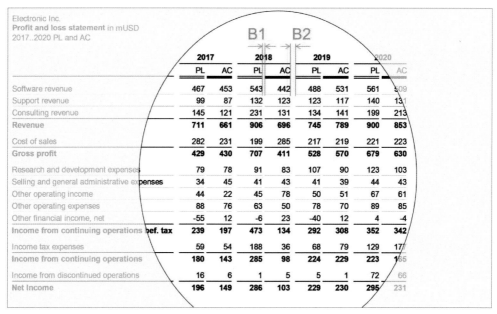

Electronic Inc.
Profit and loss statement in mUSD
2017...2020 PL and AC

	2017		2018		2019		2020	
	PL	AC	PL	AC	PL	AC	PL	AC
Software revenue	467	453	543	442	488	531	561	509
Support revenue	99	87	132	123	123	117	140	131
Consulting revenue	145	121	231	131	134	141	199	213
Revenue	711	661	906	696	745	789	900	853
Cost of sales	282	231	199	285	217	219	221	223
Gross profit	429	430	707	411	528	570	679	630
Research and development expenses	79	78	91	83	107	90	123	103
Selling and general administrative expenses	34	45	41	43	41	39	44	43
Other operating income	44	22	45	78	50	51	67	61
Other operating expenses	88	76	63	50	78	70	89	85
Other financial income, net	-55	12	-6	23	-40	12	4	-4
Income from continuing operations bef. tax	239	197	473	134	292	308	352	342
Income tax expenses	59	54	188	36	68	79	129	177
Income from continuing operations	180	143	285	98	224	229	223	165
Income from discontinued operations	16	6	1	5	5	1	72	66
Net Income	196	149	286	103	229	230	295	231

Figure EX 1.2-12: Nested columns (example)

ROW TYPES

Row types are rows with similar content falling under similar row headers. Typical row types are *measure rows* (e.g. sales, cost, profit) or *structure rows* (e.g. Italy, France, UK).

The following layout principles apply to all row types:

- **Height**: Rows belonging to a row type should have an identical height (see height A in Figure EX 1.2-14 et seq.).
- **Horizontal lines**: Separating rows by light horizontal lines will increase the legibility.

Additional layout principals depend on the row types described below.

Time periods and points of time, *scenarios*, and *variances* should be displayed in columns rather than in rows.

Column header rows

Column header rows contain the header texts of the columns. In most cases, these rows are positioned at the very top of a table. In order to group columns two and more column header rows might be necessary. If necessary, abbreviate column header texts in order to fit in the preferred column width. Alternatively keep column headers short by using footnotes.

In Figure EX 1.2-13 the *column header row* uses two lines in order to fit the column header texts in the narrow columns.

Electronic Inc.
Gross profit calculation in kUSD
2021-Q1

	Net sales	Material cost	**Staff** cost	**Other** cost	**Gross profit**
Austria	3 217	1 322	1 345	325	225
Belgium	245	111	67	33	34
France	3 467	2 145	1 007	225	90
Germany	8 754	4 566	2 389	1 678	121
Poland	3 411	1 899	1 087	347	78
Sweden	1 987	1 210	789	121	-133
Switzerland	499	234	113	34	118
Other	8 765	4 509	2 347	561	1 348
Europe	30 345	15 996	9 144	3 324	1 881

Figure EX 1.2-13: Column header row (example)

Measure rows

Measure rows show measures such as sales, headcount, or equity.

Separate rows showing final or intermediate results of a calculation scheme (*results rows*) by solid lines. Like *totals rows* (see below), the design of *results rows* should be consistent and different from other rows. The numbers are usually highlighted by bold fonts and the background can be filled e.g. by light gray if helpful. An additional gap B below a results row will increase legibility (see Figure EX 1.2-14).

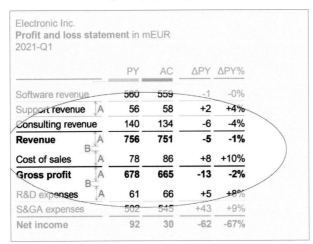

Figure EX 1.2-14: Measure rows (example)

Structure rows

Structure rows show elements of a structure dimension (e.g. countries or products).

Electronic Inc.
Net sales in mEUR
2016..2022

	2016	2017	2018	2019	2020	2021	2022
Austria	560	590	546	548	555	509	456
Belgium A	56	72	58	59	77	79	88
France	140	149	134	137	165	155	178
Germany	345	279	260	234	288	297	268
Italy	78	91	86	77	69	59	71
Sweden	77	81	86	85	93	95	98
Denmark	61	70	66	70	78	79	93
Rest of EU	502	498	545	601	688	782	655
EU	1 819	1 830	1 781	1 811	2 013	2 055	1 907

Figure EX 1.2-15: Structure row (example)

"Of which" rows

If details of an aggregated row are shown in one or more rows not totaling to the aggregated row, these rows are called "of which" rows. Place the aggregated row *above* the "of which" rows (in contrast to the *totals row* positioned *below* the rows of its group).

Use a consistent design for *of which rows* that differs from other rows. E.g. in Figure EX 1.2-16, the *of which row* is of smaller height, written in a smaller font (see X), not separated by a horizontal line, and has a right-aligned row header.

Electronic Inc.
Net sales in mEUR
2017..2022

	2017	2018	2019	2020	2021	2022
Austria	590	546	548	555	509	456
Belgium A	72	58	59	77	79	88
Germany A	149	134	137	165	155	178
of which Bavaria <A	28	26	23	29	30	27
Poland	91	86	77	69	59	71
Sweden	81	86	85	93	95	98
Switzerland	70	66	70	78	79	93
Other	498	545	601	688	782	655
Europe	1 551	1 521	1 577	1 725	1 758	1 639

Figure EX 1.2-16: "Of which" row (example)

Remainder rows

If the structure dimension to be presented in the rows outline has too many elements, accumulate the less important or smaller elements in a *remainder row* (e.g. 7 rows for the top 7 countries and a remainder titled "Rest of world").

Exclude remainder rows from some of the structure analyses such as averaging, ranking, and selecting.

In Figure EX 1.2-17, the *remainder row* has the same row height A as the other structure rows of this table example.

Electronic Inc. Net sales in mEUR 2016..2022	2016	2017	2018	2019	2020	2021	2022
Austria	560	590	546	548	555	509	456
Belgium	56	72	58	59	77	79	88
France	140	149	134	137	165	155	178
Germany	345	279	260	234	288	297	268
Italy	78	91	86	77	69	59	71
Sweden	77	81	86	85	93	95	98
Denmark	61	70	66	70	78	79	93
Rest of EU	A 502	498	545	601	688	782	655
EU	1 819	1 830	1 781	1 811	2 013	2 055	1 907

Figure EX 1.2-17: Remainder row (example)

"Percent of" rows

Use *"Percent of"* rows to present important data of another row as shares of a given total. A typical example for a *"percent of"* row is gross profit as a percentage of sales, see Figure EX 1.2-18.

"Percent of" rows have a smaller font size (see X) than the other rows.

Electronic Inc.
Gross profit calculation in mUSD
2020

	Q1	Q2	Q3	Q4	**2020**
Software	453	467	442	543	1 905
Support	87	99	123	132	441
Consulting	121	145	131	231	628
Sales	661	711	696	906	2 974
Cost of sales	231	282	285	199	997
Gross profit	**430**	**429**	**411**	**707**	**1 977**
% of sales	*65,1*	*60,3*	*59,1*	*78,0*	*66,5*

Figure EX 1.2-18: "Percent of" row (example)

Totals rows

Place rows displaying *totals of a group of rows* (e.g. countries totaling in regions or products totaling in product groups) below the rows of this group and separated them by solid lines.

The design of the *totals rows* should be consistent and different from other rows. The numbers are usually highlighted by bold fonts and the background can be filled e.g. by light gray if helpful (see Figure EX 1.2-19).

Electronic Inc.
Net sales in mEUR
2016..2022

	2016	2017	2018	2019	2020	2021	2022
Austria	560	590	546	548	555	509	456
Belgium	56	72	58	59	77	79	88
France	140	149	134	137	165	155	178
Germany	345	279	260	234	288	297	268
Italy	78	91	86	77	69	59	71
Sweden	77	81	86	85	93	95	98
Denmark	61	70	66	70	78	79	93
Rest of EU	502	498	545	601	688	782	655
EU	**1 819**	**1 830**	**1 781**	**1 811**	**2 013**	**2 055**	**1 907**

Figure EX 1.2-19: Totals row (example)

The row types described before refer to *single* rows. The following paragraphs present *combined* rows i.e. *hierarchical* and *nested* rows.

Hierarchical rows

Hierarchies in dimensions may call for rows showing multiple levels. If possible, the sibling elements belonging to the same parent element of a dimension should be homogenous, mutually exclusive, and collectively exhaustive. The principles for structuring hierarchies are covered in the chapter "STRUCTURE - Organize content".

Separate parents by appropriate means, e.g. wider gaps (see additional gap B in Figure EX 1.2-20). Display the parent rows *below* their child rows (like *totals rows*).

Electronic Inc.
Profit after tax in kEUR
Nov 2020

| | | Nov | | | | | | | | Jan_Nov | | | | | |
PY	PL	AC	ΔPY	ΔPY%	ΔPL	ΔPL%		PY	PL	AC	ΔPY	ΔPY%	ΔPL	ΔPL%
560	590	559	-1	-0%	-31	-5%	Austria	5 078	5 611	5 509	+431	+8%	-102	-2%
56	72	58	+2	+4%	-14	-19%	Belgium	531	529	484	-47	-9%	-45	-9%
140	149	134	-6	-4%	-15	-10%	France	1 290	1 488	1 354	+64	+5%	-134	-9%
345	279	260	-85	-25%	-19	-7%	Germany	3 124	2 815	2 850	-274	-9%	+35	+1%
78	91	86	+8	+10%	-5	-5%	Poland	816	818	854	+38	+5%	+36	+4%
77	81	86	+9	+12%	+5	+6%	Sweden	669	722	764	-45	-6%	+42	+6%
61	70	66	+5	+8%	-4	-6%	Switzerland	604	582	678	+74	+12%	+96	+16%
502	498	545	+43	+9%	+47	+9%	Other	5 602	6 022	5 441	-161	-3%	-581	-10%
1 819	1 830	1 794	-25	-1%	-36	-2%	Europe	17 854	18 587	17 934	+80	+0%	-653	-4%
119	109	121	+2	+2%	+12	+11%	Brazil	1 205	1 254	1 314	+109	+9%	+60	+5%
65	71	59	-6	-9%	-12	-17%	Canada	629	656	718	+89	+14%	+62	+9%
346	326	311	-35	-10%	-15	-5%	USA	3 406	3 124	3 239	-167	-5%	+115	+4%
438	401	399	-39	-9%	-2	-0%	Other	4 166	4 219	4 008	-158	-4%	-211	-5%
968	907	890	-78	-8%	-17	-2%	Americas	9 406	9 253	9 279	-127	-1%	+26	+0%
54	66	62	+8	+15%	-4	-6%	Australia	517	609	588	+71	+14%	-21	-3%
266	204	231	-35	-13%	+27	+13%	China	2 107	1 925	2 399	+292	+14%	+474	+25%
9	70	11	+2	+22%	-59	-84%	Japan	67	855	144	+77	+115%	-711	-83%
234	311	255	+21	+9%	-56	-18%	Other	2 351	2 099	2 145	-206	-9%	+46	+2%
563	651	559	-4	-1%	-92	-14%	Rest of World	5 042	5 488	5 276	+234	+5%	-212	-4%
3 350	3 388	3 243	- 107	-3%	-145	-4%	World	32 302	33 328	32 489	+187	+1%	-639	-3%

Figure EX 1.2-20: Hierarchical rows (example)

Nested rows

In *nested rows*, two types of rows are combined in such a way that the rows of one type repeat iteratively within every row of the other row type.

Separate the resulting groups of rows by appropriate means, e.g. wider gaps (see additional gap B in Figure EX 1.2-21).

Electronic Inc.
Profit after tax in kEUR
Nov 2020

PY	PL	AC	ΔPY	ΔPY%	ΔPL	ΔPL%		PY	PL	AC	ΔPY	ΔPY%	ΔPL	ΔPL%
560	590	559	-1	-0%	-31	-5%	Licences	5 078	5 611	5 509	+431	+8%	-102	-2%
56	72	58	+2	+4%	-14	-19%	Services	531	529	484	-47	-9%	-45	-9%
140	149	134	-6	-4%	-15	-10%	Consulting	1 290	1 488	1 354	+64	+5%	-134	-9%
756	**811**	**751**	**-5**	**-1%**	**-60**	**-7%**	**EMEA**	**6 899**	**7 628**	**7 347**	**+448**	**+6%**	**-281**	**-4%**
78	91	86	+8	+10%	-5	-5%	Licences	816	818	854	+38	+5%	+36	+4%
77	81	86	+9	+12%	+5	+6%	Services	809	722	764	-45	-6%	+42	+6%
61	70	66	+5	+8%	-4	-6%	Consulting	604	562	678	+74	+12%	+96	+16%
216	**242**	**238**	**+22**	**+10%**	**-4**	**-2%**	**North America**	**2 229**	**2 122**	**2 296**	**+67**	**+3%**	**+174**	**+8%**
344	13	21	+9	+75%	+8	+62%	Licences	234	2 441	289	+55	+24%	-23	-7%
119	109	121	+2	+2%	+12	+11%	Services	1 205	1 254	1 314	+109	+9%	+60	+5%
65	71	59	-6	-9%	-12	-17%	Consulting	629	656	718	+89	+14%	+62	+9%
196	**193**	**201**	**+5**	**+3%**	**+8**	**+4%**	**South America**	**2 068**	**2 222**	**2 321**	**+253**	**+12%**	**+99**	**+4%**
438	401	399	-39	-9%	-2	-0%	Licences	4 166	4 219	3 887	-279	-7%	-332	-8%
356	299	342	-22	-5%	+21	+5%	Services	3 561	3 880	3 301	+209	+6%	-110	-3%
119	109	121	+2	+2%	+12	+11%	Consulting	1 205	1 254	1 314	+109	+9%	+60	+5%
988	**898**	**929**	**-59**	**-6%**	**+31**	**+3%**	**Asia**	**8 932**	**9 353**	**8 971**	**+39**	**+0%**	**-382**	**-4%**
266	204	231	-35	-13%	+27	+13%	Licences	2 327	1 925	2 107	-220	-9%	+182	+9%
78	70	77	-1	-1%	+7	+10%	Services	825	855	916	+91	+11%	+61	+7%
234	311	255	+21	+9%	-56	-18%	Consulting	2 351	2 099	2 145	-206	-9%	+46	+2%
578	**585**	**563**	**-15**	**-3%**	**-22**	**-4%**	**Rest of World**	**5 503**	**4 879**	**5 168**	**-335**	**-6%**	**+289**	**+6%**
2 734	2 729	2 682	-52	-2%	-47	-2%	**World**	25 631	26 204	26 103	+472	+2%	-101	-0%

(Column group headers: **Nov** spans the first PY/PL/AC/ΔPY/ΔPY%/ΔPL/ΔPL% block; **Jan_Nov** spans the second block.)

B ⇕ A / ⇕ A

Figure EX 1.2-21: Nested rows (example)

TABLE TYPES

Table types are distinguished by their analytic purpose in time series tables, variance tables and cross tables, see Figure EX 1.2. Tables serving more than one analytic purpose are called combined tables.

Time **table**			Variance **table**			Cross **table**		
	'19	'20		PL AC ΔPL			Sales	Profit
Italy			Italy			Italy		
Austria			Austria			Austria		
UK			UK			UK		
France			France			France		
Rest			Rest			Rest		
Europe			**Europe**			**Europe**		

Figure EX 1.2: Use appropriate table types

Time series tables

Time series tables are used for time series analyses, combining time columns with measure rows or structure rows.

A typical example for a *time series table* is a sales analysis by countries (rows) and years (columns), see Figure EX 1.2-22.

Electronic Inc.
Net sales in mEUR
2010..2016

	2016	2017	2018	2019	2020	2021	2022
Austria	560	590	546	548	555	509	456
Belgium	56	72	58	59	77	79	88
France	140	149	134	137	165	155	178
Germany	345	279	260	234	288	297	268
Italy	78	91	86	77	69	59	71
Sweden	77	81	86	85	93	95	98
Denmark	61	70	66	70	78	79	93
Rest of EU	502	498	545	601	688	782	655
EU	**1 819**	**1 830**	**1 781**	**1 811**	**2 013**	**2 055**	**1 907**

Figure EX 1.2-22: Time series table (example)

Variance tables

Variance tables are used for scenario analyses, combining scenario columns and variance columns with measure rows or structure rows.

A typical example for a *variance table* is a sales analysis by countries (rows) showing different scenarios and different variances (columns), see Figure EX 1.2-23.

```
Electronic Inc.
Net sales in mEUR
2021-Q1
```

	PY	PL	AC	ΔPY	ΔPY%	ΔPL	ΔPL%
Austria	560	590	559	-1	-0%	-31	-5%
Belgium	56	72	58	+2	+4%	-14	-19%
France	140	149	134	-6	-4%	-15	-10%
Germany	345	279	260	-85	-25%	-19	-7%
Poland	78	91	86	+8	+10%	-5	-5%
Sweden	77	81	86	+9	+12%	+5	+6%
Italy	61	70	66	+5	+8%	-4	-6%
Other	502	498	545	+43	+9%	+47	+9%
Europe	**1 819**	**1 830**	**1 794**	**-25**	**-1%**	**-36**	**-2%**

Figure EX 1.2-23: Variance table (example)

Cross tables

Cross tables are used for structure analyses, combining structure columns with structure rows.

A typical example of a *cross table* is a sales table with countries in rows and products in columns, see Figure EX 1.2-24.

```
Electronic Inc.
Net sales in mEUR
2021-Q1
```

	AL1	AL2	AL3	AL4	AL5	AL6..9	AL
Austria	231	590	432	559	123	559	**2 494**
Belgium	23	72	58	33	6	58	**250**
France	55	149	134	134	134	134	**740**
Germany	762	210	100	43	15	29	**1 159**
Poland	56	91	7	77	82	55	**368**
Sweden	74	81	41	44	123	341	**704**
Denmark	32	70	66	43	52	25	**288**
Other	502	498	127	321	776	321	**2 545**
Europe	**1 735**	**1 761**	**965**	**1 254**	**1 311**	**1 522**	**8 548**

Figure EX 1.2-24: Cross table (example)

Combined tables

Combined tables are used for multiple analyses. A combined table uses more than one *column type* and/or more than one *row type* presented either side by side or nested (see nested columns and nested rows).

Figure EX 1.2-25 shows a hierarchical structure of countries on three levels in the rows. The columns are nested: scenarios and variances are the same for both time periods *November* and *January_November*.

Electronic Inc.
Profit after tax in kEUR
Nov 2020

		Nov								Jan_Nov					
PY	PL	AC	ΔPY	ΔPY%	ΔPL	ΔPL%		PY	PL	AC	ΔPY	ΔPY%	ΔPL	ΔPL%
560	590	559	-1	-0%	-31	-5%	Austria	5 078	5 611	5 509	+431	+8%	-102	-2%
56	72	58	+2	+4%	-14	-19%	Belgium	531	529	484	-47	-9%	-45	-9%
140	149	134	-6	-4%	-15	-10%	France	1 290	1 488	1 354	+64	+5%	-134	-9%
345	279	260	-85	-25%	-19	-7%	Germany	3 124	2 815	2 850	-274	-9%	+35	+1%
78	91	86	+8	+10%	-5	-5%	Poland	816	818	854	+38	+5%	+36	+4%
77	81	86	+9	+12%	+5	+6%	Sweden	809	722	764	-45	-6%	+42	+6%
61	70	66	+5	+8%	-4	-6%	Switzerland	604	582	678	+74	+12%	+96	+16%
502	498	545	+43	+9%	+47	+9%	Other	5 602	6 022	5 441	-161	-3%	-581	-10%
1 819	**1 830**	**1 794**	**-25**	**-1%**	**-36**	**-2%**	**Europe**	**17 854**	**18 587**	**17 934**	**+80**	**+0%**	**-653**	**-4%**
119	109	121	+2	+2%	+12	+11%	Brazil	1 205	1 254	1 314	+109	+9%	+60	+5%
65	71	59	-6	-9%	-12	-17%	Canada	629	656	718	+89	+14%	+62	+9%
346	326	311	-35	-10%	-15	-5%	USA	3 406	3 124	3 239	-167	-5%	+115	+4%
438	401	399	-39	-9%	-2	-0%	Other	4 166	4 219	4 008	-158	-4%	-211	-5%
968	**907**	**890**	**-78**	**-8%**	**-17**	**-2%**	**Americas**	**9 406**	**9 253**	**9 279**	**-127**	**-1%**	**+26**	**+0%**
54	66	62	+8	+15%	-4	-6%	Australia	517	609	588	+71	+14%	-21	-3%
266	204	231	-35	-13%	+27	+13%	China	2 107	1 925	2 399	+292	+14%	+474	+25%
9	70	11	+2	+22%	-59	-84%	Japan	67	855	144	+77	+115%	-711	-83%
234	311	255	+21	+9%	-56	-18%	Other	2 351	2 099	2 145	-206	-9%	+46	+2%
563	**651**	**559**	**-4**	**-1%**	**-92**	**-14%**	**Rest of World**	**5 042**	**5 488**	**5 276**	**+234**	**+5%**	**-212**	**-4%**
3 350	**3 388**	**3 243**	**- 107**	**-3%**	**-145**	**-4%**	**World**	**32 302**	**33 328**	**32 489**	**+187**	**+1%**	**-839**	**-3%**

Figure EX 1.2-25: Combined table (example 1)

Figure EX 1.2-26 shows the measures of a calculation scheme in the rows. The columns are nested: The four quarters and the annual total are the same for both years.

Electronic Inc.
Profit and loss statement in mUSD
2019, 2020

	Q1	Q2	Q3	Q4	2019	Q1	Q2	Q3	Q4	2020
Software revenue	453	467	442	543	1 905	531	488	509	561	2 089
Support revenue	87	99	123	132	441	117	123	131	140	511
Consulting revenue	121	145	131	231	628	141	134	213	199	687
Revenue	**661**	**711**	**696**	**906**	**2 974**	**789**	**745**	**853**	**900**	**3 287**
Cost of sales	231	282	285	199	997	219	217	223	221	880
Gross profit	**430**	**429**	**411**	**707**	**1 977**	**570**	**528**	**630**	**679**	**2 407**
Research and development expenses	78	79	83	91	331	90	107	103	123	423
Selling and general administrative expenses	45	34	43	41	163	39	41	43	44	167
Other operating income	22	44	78	45	189	51	50	61	67	229
Other operating expenses	76	88	50	63	277	70	78	85	89	322
Other financial income, net	12	-55	23	-6	-26	12	-40	-4	4	-28
Income from continuing operations bef. tax	**197**	**239**	**134**	**473**	**1 043**	**308**	**292**	**342**	**352**	**1 294**
Income tax expenses	54	59	36	188	337	79	68	177	129	453
Income from continuing operations	**143**	**180**	**98**	**285**	**706**	**229**	**224**	**165**	**223**	**841**
Income from discontinued operations	6	16	5	1	28	1	5	66	72	144
Net Income	**149**	**196**	**103**	**286**	**734**	**230**	**229**	**231**	**295**	**985**

Figure EX 1.2-26: Combined table (example 2)

Figure EX 1.2-27 shows the same rows as the second one (measures of a calculation scheme). The nested columns now show PY and AC data as well as absolute and relative variances for two markets.

Electronic Inc.
Profit and loss statement in mUSD
2020

	PY		AC		ΔPY		ΔPY%	
	Home	Intern.	Home	Intern.	Home	Intern.	Home	Intern.
Software revenue	265	809	244	906	-21	+97	-8%	+12%
Support revenue	87	244	88	255	+1	+11	+1%	+5%
Consulting revenue	121	388	114	340	-7	-48	-6%	-12%
Revenue	**473**	**1 441**	**446**	**1 501**	**-27**	**+60**	**-6%**	**+4%**
Cost of sales	122	477	134	450	+12	-27	+10%	-6%
Gross profit	**351**	**964**	**312**	**1 051**	**-39**	**+87**	**-11%**	**+9%**
Research and development expenses	78	223	88	240	+10	+17	+13%	+8%
Selling and general administrative expenses	97	307	99	298	+2	-9	+2%	-3%
Other operating income	22	45	52	145	+30	+100	+136%	+222%
Other operating expenses	76	45	62	55	-14	+10	-18%	+22%
Other financial income (expenses), net	12	-5	23	- 8	+11	-3	+92%	+60%
Income from continuing operations bef. tax	**66**	**349**	**-12**	**321**	**-78**	**-28**	**-118%**	**-8%**
Income tax expenses	23	122	27	129	+4	+7	+17%	+6%
Income from continuing operations	**43**	**227**	**-39**	**192**	**-82**	**-35**	**-191%**	**-15%**
Income from discontinued operations	56	66	66	72	+10	+6	+18%	+9%
Net Income	**99**	**293**	**27**	**264**	**-72**	**-29**	**-73%**	**-10%**

Figure EX 1.2-27: Combined table (example 3)

EX 2   REPLACE INAPPROPRIATE CHART TYPES

Inappropriate charts make it hard to perceive the message. Knowing the correct usage of chart types helps in replacing inappropriate visualizations, such as pie charts, speedometer visualizations, radar charts, and spaghetti charts, with those chart types better suited.

EX 2.1   REPLACE PIE AND RING CHARTS

Pie and *ring charts* are circular charts dividing some total into sectors of relative proportion, but there are better ways to illustrate the numerical proportions of segments, e.g. bar charts or charts with stacked columns, see Figure EX 2.1.

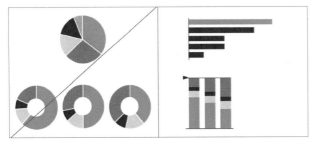

Figure EX 2.1: Replace pie and ring charts

Pie charts allow for one-dimensional analyses only, and therefore seldom convey revealing insights. However, some useful applications for pie charts exist, for example when market sizes and/or market shares for one period need to be allocated to certain regions on a map (see the CHECK rule CH 3.3 "Avoid misleading colored areas in maps"). As opposed to column or bar charts, pie charts can be positioned on a specific point on a map.

EX 2.2   REPLACE GAUGES, SPEEDOMETERS

Often found as part of a dashboard, *speedometers* can usually be replaced by more suitable visualizations. They have been invented for monitoring real-time information which is rarely included in management reporting. They also take up way too much space and have often confusing color coding and scaling. In general, bar charts showing the respective structures or columns charts showing the respective development over time are better choices, see Figure EX 2.2.

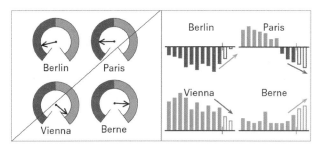

Figure EX 2.2: Replace gauges, speedometers

EX 2.3 REPLACE RADAR AND FUNNEL CHARTS

So-called *radar charts* (also called *net charts* or *spider charts*) are frequently used for evaluating purposes. Having no advantage over bar charts and having, actually, many weaknesses, use them only for two-dimensional analyses (e.g. comparing young-old with rich-poor). Willard C. Brinton wrote almost 100 years ago[16]: "This type of chart should be banished to the scrap heap. Charts on rectangular ruling are easier to draw and easier to understand."

Of course, if the circular arrangement of categories has meaning (such as the compass direction), this kind of chart can be very valuable, but these types of analysis are not typical in business reporting.

Funnel charts are misleading when the size of the area displayed does not correspond to the respective numerical values – an issue applying also to other artificial chart forms (e.g. spheres) in which the length, area, or volume do not correspond to the numerical values.

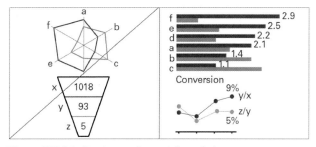

Figure EX 2.3: Replace radar and funnel charts

---

[16] Brinton, Willard C.: Graphic Methods for Presenting Facts, 1914(!), page 80

EX 2.4 REPLACE SPAGHETTI CHARTS

A chart with more than three or four intersecting lines ("spaghetti chart") can be more confusing than several smaller charts with one line each placed next to one another (small multiples), particularly when evaluating the shape or the trend of the lines, see Figure EX 2.4.

However, when needing to compare exactly the height of data points of several lines, spaghetti charts cannot be avoided.

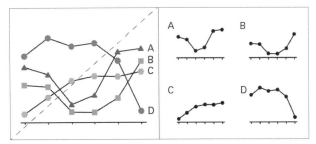

Figure EX 2.4: Replace spaghetti charts

EX 2.5 REPLACE TRAFFIC LIGHTS

"Traffic lights" with green, red, and yellow areas are a popular form of visualization but contain little information per area used. However, they can be used for analyses showing "yes or no" decisions or situations similar to real traffic lights. In all other cases replace them with more suitable means of (analog) representation such as bar charts, see Figure EX 2.5.

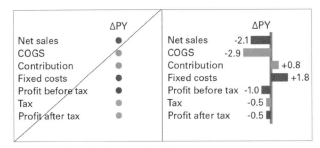

Figure EX 2.5: Replace traffic lights

EX 3 REPLACE INAPPROPRIATE REPRESENTATIONS

From a perceptual perspective, avoid all visual representations requiring time consuming analyses or additional explanations, particularly the popular use of merely conceptual representations and all forms of texts, including bullet lists.

EX 3.1   PREFER QUANTITATIVE REPRESENTATIONS

Due to the time constraints usually involved with presentations, conceptual graphs prove less suitable than charts, photos, maps, etc. For a one-hour presentation, do not use more than three or four conceptual representations. Do this only if they are absolutely essential for comprehension. The audience will understand charts and pictures (photos, drawings, etc.) better and faster, see Figure EX 3.1.

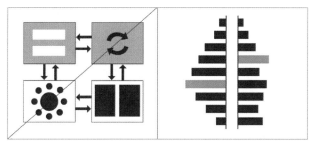

Figure EX 3.1: Prefer quantitative representations

EX 3.2   AVOID TEXT SLIDES IN PRESENTATIONS

Avoid all forms of text slides in presentations. Texts should either be recited or written in a handout. A few exceptions to this rule are specific texts being discussed such as definitions, quotes, etc. In general, all forms of lists (bullet points) should appear only in the written handout, not projected on the screen. True, if someone sees and hears something simultaneously, he remembers it better than when he just hears it, but bear in mind texts are not considered something merely to be seen – they must be read and understood, see Figure EX 3.2.

Figure EX 3.2: Avoid text slides in presentations

EX 4   ADD COMPARISONS

Visual perception is strongly based on setting one perceived object in relation to another. Adding meaningful comparisons helps the eye evaluate faster, the main purpose of charts.

EX 4.1 ADD SCENARIOS

Scenarios such as "plan" and "previous year" are the most common references for comparison purposes. Add them whenever available. Use a standardized scenario notation for faster comprehension, see Figure EX 4.1.

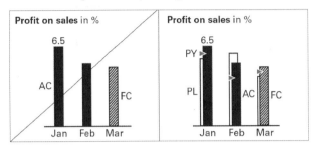

Figure EX 4.1: Add scenarios

EX 4.2 ADD VARIANCES

Having added scenarios for comparison purposes, the visualization of variances makes it easier to evaluate the situation. Use a standardized notation of variances for faster comprehension, see Figure EX 4.2.

Figure EX 4.2: Add variances

EX 5 EXPLAIN CAUSES

Present data more understandable by showing interrelations, i.e. causes and dependencies. Seeing the entire context, especially extreme values and deviant values, helps to explain causes. Details increase not only the level of credibility but also comprehension. Use charts to prove, explain, and render something plausible, not to serve merely as decoration.

This section focuses on the explanation of causes by using tree structures, clusters, and correlations. A more structured approach to increasing information density is discussed in the chapter "CONDENSE – Increase information density".

EX 5.1 SHOW TREE STRUCTURES

The presentation of the assumptions or basic data upon which a business analysis is based, results not only in better understanding, but also makes it more convincing. A good choice is the display of calculated measures in a tree structure, see Figure EX 5.1 (see also the CONDENSE rule CO 5.2 "Show related charts on one page").

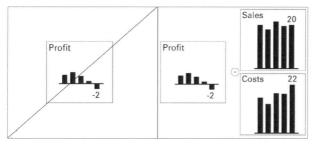

Figure EX 5.1: Show tree structures

EX 5.2 SHOW CLUSTERS

With the help of clusters in two-dimensional and three-dimensional forms, large amounts of data very often can provide interesting and new insights, see Figure EX 5.2.

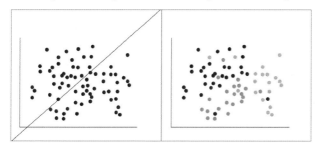

Figure EX 5.2: Show clusters

EX 5.3 SHOW CORRELATIONS

When comparing several data series, correlations are often sought in order to better understand the interrelations. Suitable rankings and comparisons can facilitate the understanding of patterns, see Figure EX 5.3.

Figure EX 5.3: Show correlations

SIMPLIFY – AVOID CLUTTER

SIMPLIFY covers all aspects of avoiding clutter in reports, presentations and dashboards.

Avoiding clutter means that reports avoid all components and characteristics, which are too complicated, redundant, distracting or merely decorative.

This chapter covers avoiding unnecessary and decorative components and replacing them with cleaner layouts, avoiding redundancies and distracting details. Many of these rules will become obsolete if we use the IBCS notation presented in the UNIFY chapter right from the beginning. We do need them to revise existing reports though.

SI 1   AVOID UNNECESSARY COMPONENTS

Completely avoid components, such as pictures, backgrounds, and logos, not contributing to the comprehension of reports, presentations or dashboards.

SI 1.1   AVOID CLUTTERED LAYOUTS

Layout concepts often contain elements that lack meaning but merely conform to corporate design or personal taste. Avoid all these elements, see Figure SI 1.1.

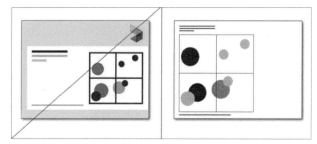

Figure SI 1.1: Avoid cluttered layouts

SI 1.2   AVOID COLORED OR FILLED BACKGROUNDS

Numbers and labels are easiest to read when depicted in black on a white background. Any type of background color or pattern makes something harder to read, see Figure SI 1.2.

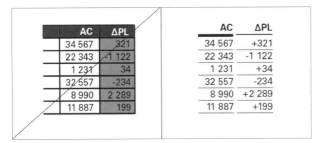

Figure SI 1.2: Avoid colored or filled backgrounds

SI 1.3 AVOID ANIMATION AND TRANSITION EFFECTS

Animated *PowerPoint* slides are not useful if the animation has no meaning and does not support the message, see Figure SI 1.3. They merely distract and confuse. Only the "appear" function is recommended to be used for the gradual development of a slide.

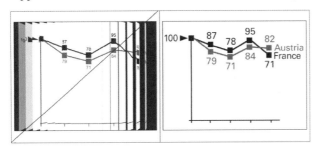

Figure SI 1.3: Avoid animation and transition effects

SI 2 AVOID DECORATIVE STYLES

Simplify complicated visualizations in order to facilitate and accelerate their comprehension. Whereas the section "Avoid unnecessary components" involves omitting entire layout elements, the aim here is to find the most suitable and simplest possible style of visualization elements.

SI 2.1 AVOID FRAMES, SHADES, AND PSEUDO-3D WITHOUT MEANING

In general, frames, shades, and pseudo-3D convey no meaning and make comprehension more difficult. Shades and pseudo-3D might even give a false visual impression. Avoid them because they do not add value, see Figure SI 2.1.

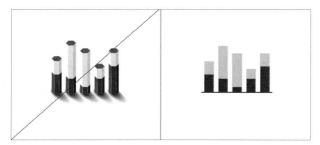
Figure SI 2.1: Avoid frames, shades, and pseudo-3D

SI 2.2 AVOID DECORATIVE COLORS

If colors serve merely decorative purpose in one instance, using them for meaning in another instance (e.g. for highlighting) becomes difficult. Therefore use colors only if they convey meaning, see Figure SI 2.2.

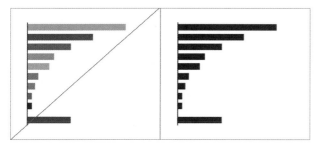
Figure SI 2.2: Avoid decorative colors

SI 2.3 AVOID DECORATIVE FONTS

A normal typeface and clear fonts increase legibility. Save bold and cursive fonts for making distinctions, see Figure SI 2.3.

Figure SI 2.3: Avoid decorative fonts

SI 3   REPLACE WITH CLEANER LAYOUT

Using a cleaner method of visualization decreases the amount of ink necessary to convey a message.

SI 3.1   REPLACE GRID LINES AND VALUE AXES WITH DATA LABELS

Using integrated data labels can make value axes, tick marks, and gridlines superfluous, see Figure SI 3.1. Gridlines, however, can be useful in charts with missing reference points as might be the case in charts with many data series and data points, or in small charts (e.g. small multiples).

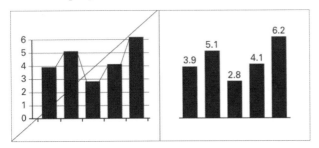

Figure SI 3.1: Replace grid lines and value axes with data labels

SI 3.2   AVOID VERTICAL LINES BY RIGHT-ALIGNING DATA

Omit all avoidable elements to make tables more straightforward. Avoid vertical lines by right-aligning numerical values and the corresponding column headers, see Figure SI 3.2.

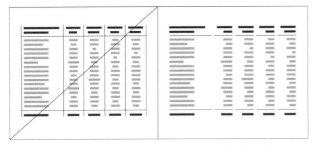

Figure SI 3.2: Avoid vertical lines by right-aligning data

SI 4   AVOID REDUNDANCIES

Avoiding redundant terms usually increases the legibility of charts and tables. In some cases, a certain amount of redundancy can be helpful like when the time period named in the chart title also appears in said chart. But unnecessary redundancy impedes comprehension like when naming the year twelve times in a chart with twelve monthly category labels.

SI 4.1   AVOID SUPERFLUOUS EXTRA WORDS

Extra words such as "sum" and "total" are redundant because they add no value to the meaning of the term they accompany. No difference exists between "Europe" and "Sum of Europe". Extra words make it harder to read text elements, see Figure SI 4.1.

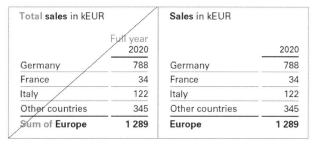

Figure SI 4.1: Avoid superfluous extra words

SI 4.2   AVOID OBVIOUS TERMS

Terms such as "chart analysis", "development", or "comment" are redundant because they name something already shown, see Figure SI 4.2. Other obvious terms in charts and tables are "table", "statistics", "report", "visualization", "structure", or "trend".

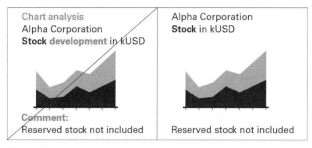

Figure SI 4.2: Avoid obvious terms

SI 4.3   AVOID REPEATED WORDS

Repeated words in legends, axis labels, row headers, etc. such as "division" in "division A", "division B", etc. or "2020" in "Q1 2020", "Q2 2020", etc. should be avoided, see Figure SI 4.3. Omitting repeated words usually increases the degree of legibility.

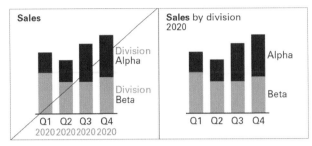

Figure SI 4.3: Avoid repeated words

SI 5   AVOID DISTRACTING DETAILS

In addition to avoiding noise and redundancy, omitting nonessential, distracting information details facilitates comprehension. Examples include unnecessarily large numbers and disproportionately detailed information in project or product overviews.

SI 5.1   AVOID LABELS FOR SMALL VALUES

Labels of small values are often hard to position and rarely contribute to the comprehension of the message. Therefore they can be avoided in most cases, see Figure SI 5.1. However, add them when special reference is made to them. If it is necessary to label these small values or small visualization elements, *assisting lines* might be necessary.

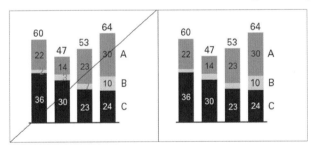

Figure SI 5.1: Avoid labels for small values

SI 5.2   AVOID LONG NUMBERS

Numbers with more than three digits in charts and four digits in tables are hard to read; moreover, such precision is seldom necessary to understand the message, see Figure SI 5.2.

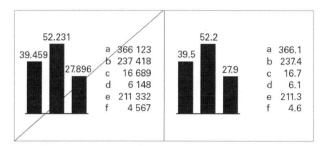

Figure SI 5.2: Avoid long numbers

SI 5.3 AVOID UNNECESSARY LABELS

Omit labels for data points that do not represent extreme values or values of special importance, see Figure SI 5.3.

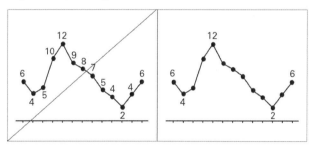

Figure SI 5.3: Avoid unnecessary labels

CONDENSE – INCREASE INFORMATION DENSITY

CONDENSE covers all aspects of increasing information density in reports, presentations and dashboards.

Increasing information density means that all reports include all information that is necessary to understand the respective message on one page. Applying a consistent semantic notation as suggested in the UNIFY chapter will pave the way for such highly condensed reports.

This chapter covers using small components, utilizing space, as well as adding data, elements, and objects.

CO 1   USE SMALL COMPONENTS

The need for a higher level of information density requires to display all objects, elements, and signs as small as possible, while still being legible. Different technical parameters apply to printed material, screen displays, and projected slides.

CO 1.1   USE SMALL FONTS

In general, avoid oversize fonts. They needlessly waste space, see Figure CO 1.1.

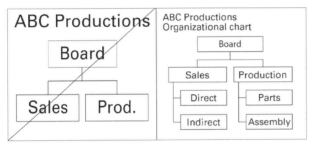

Figure CO 1.1: Use small fonts

CO 1.2   USE SMALL ELEMENTS

Small elements increase clarity. Large-scale symbols and highlights are not more suitable than smaller symbols and highlights, see Figure CO 1.2.

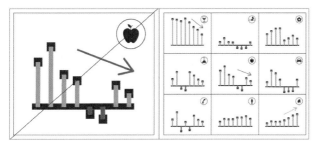

Figure CO 1.2: Use small elements

CO 1.3 USE SMALL OBJECTS

The size of charts and tables in reports and presentations should not be as large as possible, rather as small as possible – yet only so small so that the objects and all its details and labels can be read easily. This provides room for more information and therefore better understanding of the context, see Figure CO 1.3.

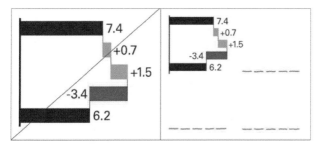

Figure CO 1.3: Use small objects

CO 2 MAXIMIZE USE OF SPACE

Utilizing free space is the fastest and easiest way to increase information density. Make better use of needlessly wide margins and frames, or blank or little used pages by filling them with helpful data pertaining to the context.

CO 2.1 USE NARROW PAGE MARGINS

The page layout is often dominated by corporate design standards not made for high information density but for attractive design, sacrificing valuable space to layout elements such as extra wide page margins, see Figure CO 2.1.

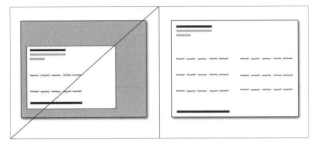

Figure CO 2.1: Use narrow page margins

CO 2.2 REDUCE EMPTY SPACE

Reduce empty space to increase information density. This applies not only to the page layout (see Figure CO 2.1) but also to the layout of report objects such as charts and tables (see Figure CO 2.2).

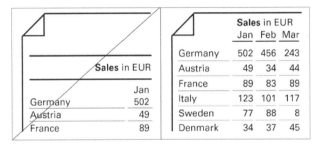

Figure CO 2.2: Reduce empty space

CO 3 ADD DATA

Adding more data to an existing visualization increases information density and helps better understand the context.

CO 3.1 ADD DATA POINTS

Displaying more data points does not jeopardize the comprehension of numerical data. For example, a monthly statistic of staff numbers over twelve months in a year would be understood just as quickly as for the same data series with twelve months for each of the last three years – in other words, a total of 36 data points instead of twelve. Usually, interesting relationships are only detected with an increased number of elements in a data series (see Figure CO 3.1).

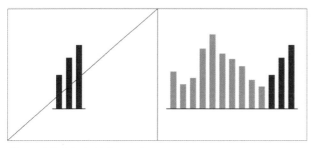

Figure CO 3.1: Add data points

CO 3.2 ADD DIMENSIONS

A very useful way to increase information density is to show more than two dimensions of a business situation. A chart with only one dimension (such as in a pie chart), visualizes only mundane things easily stated in a simple sentence. Already charts with two dimensions can yield very interesting relationships – yet those charts with three and more dimensions yield structures leading to completely new insights (see Figure CO 3.2).

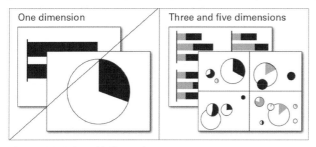

Figure CO 3.2: Add dimensions

CO 4 ADD ELEMENTS

It is often appropriate to use two or more basic chart types (either horizontal or vertical) to build *combined charts* with a higher information density. *Combined charts* are treated as one entity as opposed to multiple charts. *Combined charts* can be built both out from horizontal or vertical charts.

There are three types of combined charts depending on their type of combination: *Overlay charts*, *multi-tier charts*, and *extended charts*. Additionally, chart elements can be embedded in tables and explanations can be integrated.

CO 4.1 SHOW OVERLAY CHARTS

In an *overlay chart*, two or more basic charts overlap. These overlapping charts always use the same category axis.

Overlay charts can facilitate comprehension such as in the combination of the development of sales (a series of columns) and the return on sales in percent (a line). However, this approach can only be used for a few chart combinations, see Figure CO 4.1.

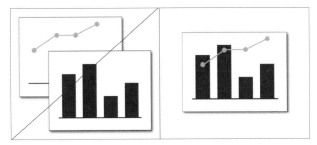

Figure CO 4.1: Show overlay charts

Overlay charts frequently use different value axes. A *column chart* representing a measure (e.g. sales) combined with a *line chart* representing another measure (e.g. employees) is a typical example (see Figure CO 4.1-1).

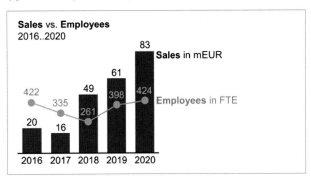

Figure CO 4.1-1: Overlay chart with lines and columns using *different* value axes (example)

Sometimes, the same value axis is used as well. A *column chart* representing a measure (e.g. sales per capita) combined with a *line chart* representing a different perspective of the same measure (e.g. industry average) is a typical example for such an *overlay chart* (see Figure CO 4.1-2).

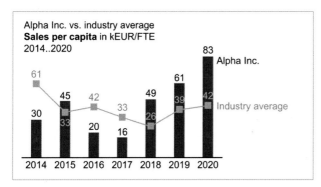

Figure CO 4.1-2: Overlay chart with columns and lines using the *same* value axis(example)

Column or bar charts with *integrated variances* (variances displayed within the columns or bars) are other typical example for *overlay charts* using the same value axis (see Figure CO 4.1-3 and Figure CO 4.1-4). Compared to two-tier charts, this presentation of two data series uses much less space. The disadvantages, though, are twofold: First, it is difficult to label the data of both the primary and secondary chart. Second, the development over time (horizontal axis) respectively the structure (vertical axis) of the primary chart is difficult to see.

Suggestion: If there is enough space, use multi-tier charts instead.

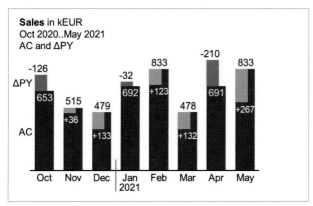

Figure CO 4.1-3: Overlay column chart with integrated variances (example)

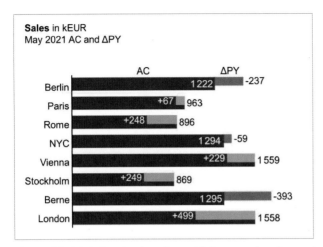

Figure CO 4.1-4: Overlay bar chart with integrated variances (example)

CO 4.2 SHOW MULTI-TIER CHARTS

Use *multi-tier charts* to increase information density by adding additional tiers to the same category axis for analyses on the same basic data. Multi-tier charts are most frequently used for displaying variances along with the basic values, see Figure CO 4.2.

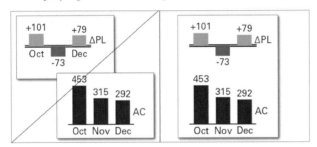

Figure CO 4.2: Show multi-tier charts

In a *two-tier chart*, a *secondary chart* is shifted in parallel to the category axis of the *primary chart*. For horizontal charts the secondary chart appears above the primary chart, for vertical charts the secondary chart appears *to the right of* the primary chart.

In both cases, the *category axes* of the primary charts are reduplicated in the secondary charts, usually having a different semantic scenario design.

Both the primary and the secondary charts have their own value axes. Value axes showing the same currency or the same physical unit should be scaled identically.

In a *three-tier chart* a third chart appears above a horizontal or to the right of a vertical two-tier chart. In special cases, more than three tiers can be combined.

Improve the interpretation of a primary chart showing grouped bars for actual and plan data by adding variances. In Figure CO 4.2-1 and Figure CO 4.2-2 a secondary chart with absolute variances and a tertiary pin chart with relative variances are combined.

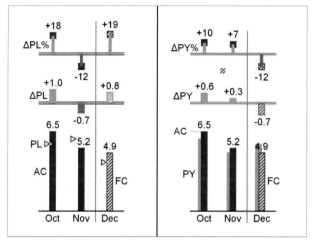

Figure CO 4.2-1: Horizontal multi-tier charts (example)

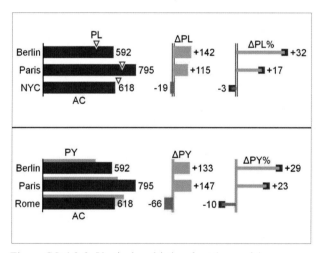

Figure CO 4.2-2: Vertical multi-tier chart (example)

CO 4.3 SHOW EXTENDED CHARTS

An *extended chart*, arranges additional charts *next* to the primary chart by virtually extending the category axis. This way of increasing information density often is used when displaying context information such as market averages or competitor figures, see Figure CO 4.3.

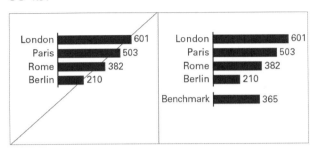

Figure CO 4.3: Show extended charts

For horizontal charts, additional charts appear to the left or right of the primary chart, for vertical charts, above or below. In both cases, position the *category axes* of the additional charts on a virtual extension of the category axes of the primary chart.

In an extended chart, use the same value axis for both the primary and the additional charts.

Improve the interpretation of a primary chart by adding extended charts showing the same values from a different perspective. In Figure CO 4.3-1, a secondary *grouped column chart* at the right hand side shows the monthly average.

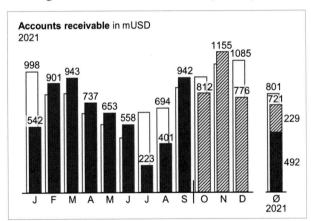

Figure CO 4.3-1: Horizontal extended chart (example)

CO 4.4 EMBED CHART ELEMENTS IN TABLES

Increase the information density of tables by using *chart elements*, see Figure CO 4.4. Bars, sparklines, and traffic lights are the predominant chart element types in tables.

Sales in kEUR 2020	PY	AC	ΔPY	Sales in kEUR 2020	PY	AC	ΔPY	
Germany	84	87	+3	Germany	84	87		+3
Austria	19	17	-2	Austria	19	17	-2	
France	28	27	-1	France	28	27	-1	
Rest	36	39	+3	Rest	36	39		+3
Europe	**167**	**170**	**+3**	**Europe**	**167**	**170**		**+3**

Figure CO 4.4: Embed chart elements in tables

TABLE BARS

Table bars are bar charts integrated into tables. The categories of these bar charts must correspond to the rows of a table. Both single bar charts with single bars or pins and waterfall bar charts are powerful means to visualize the absolute figures and variances in tables. Most recommendations concerning vertical chart types can be applied to *table bars*.

SPARKLINES

Omit *sparklines* if not scaled properly. Individually scaled sparklines can be misleading because small fluctuations in a series of other small fluctuations look the same as big fluctuations in a series of big fluctuations. However, sparklines with proper scaling (e.g. indexed) can be helpful.

TRAFFIC LIGHTS

Traffic lights contain little information, as they represent no more than three (red, green, yellow) states. Use them only if there is no more information to be conveyed than those two or three states (e.g. "yes" or "no"). In all other cases, replace traffic lights with more suitable means of representation, such as *table bars*.

CO 4.5 EMBED EXPLANATIONS

Both the density of information and the level of comprehension increase when explanations are embedded into charts and tables (this applies to written reports and handouts only).

When the explanation refers directly to the visual presentation in question, it helps to establish a connection and speeds up comprehension, see Figure CO 4.5.

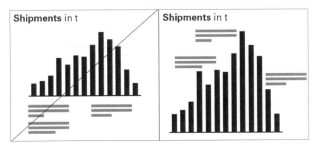

Figure CO 4.5: Embed explanations

CO 5   ADD OBJECTS

Reports and presentation material consist of one or more *pages*. The content of one page can be viewed together without referring to other content, e.g. flipping to other pages.

Reports and presentation material often arrange more than one chart on one page. While this increases information density and fosters a higher level of comparability, it presents a design challenge: A uniform notation concept and consistent scaling are even more important than on pages with single charts.

The most important types of pages with multiple objects are small multiples and multi-charts (including *ratio trees*).

CO 5.1   SHOW SMALL MULTIPLES

Substantially improve the comprehension of complex relationships by displaying charts of the same type and the same scale on the same page. These charts are called *small multiples*, see Figure CO 5.1.

Typical applications are charts with different countries, products, or projects placed next to each other. Of course, there is an upper limit to the number of charts on one page, depending mainly on the page- and font-size used.

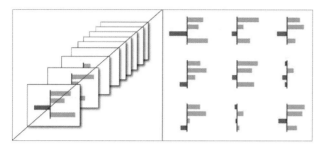

Figure CO 5.1: Show small multiples

Showing *small multiples* is a good way to compare a set of up to around 25 charts. Instead of exceeding this number on one page, a new chart called "Others" containing the accumulation of all other elements could be a solution.

As mentioned in the chapter "CHECK - Ensure visual integrity", all small multiples must use the identical scale, see Figure CO 5.1-1.

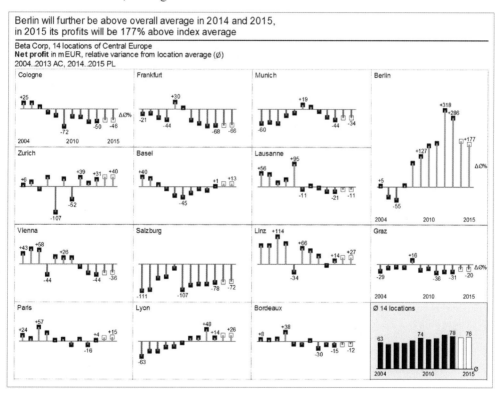

Figure CO 5.1-1: Screen page with *small multiples* (example)

Working with *small multiples* can be difficult if certain charts show significantly bigger values than others. Using a different scale for a chart with bigger values is not a feasible option, increase the size of this chart instead.

CO 5.2 SHOW RELATED CHARTS ON ONE PAGE

Different from small multiples, *related charts cover different topics (different measures) on one page*. They mostly use different scales, too. This arrangement of charts on one page is sometimes called *multi-charts*. But the term *multi-charts* fails to underline the fact that these charts must have a useful relationship. It does not make sense to arrange several, completely unrelated charts on one page.

This approach offers high data density and a higher level of comparability – but it can be a demanding visual and technical challenge as a uniform notation concept, clear terms, and an understandable scaling prove even more important (see Figure CO 5.2).

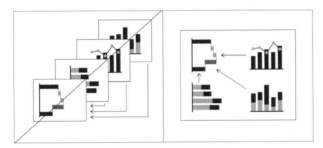

Figure CO 5.2: Show related charts on one page

Consistent scaling of *multi-charts* can be difficult. Sometimes different scales for the same unit or measure are inevitable. In this case, clearly indicate the use of a different scale by an appropriate mean, e.g. scaling indicators.

Ratio trees are multi-charts showing root causes. Use ratio trees to prove or explain a specific issue. Pointing out the assumptions and root causes of variances or temporal evolvements improves understanding and is more convincing, too. In general, the *ratio* is broken down into its components (mostly from left to right). Thus individual charts, preferably identical size, are arranged in a tree shape structure.

Consistent scaling of *ratio trees* can be difficult. Sometimes different scales for the same unit or measure are inevitable. In this case, clearly indicate the use of a different scale by an appropriate mean, e.g. scaling indicators.

A typical example of a page showing a *ratio tree* is the "Return on asset" tree, see Figure CO 5.2-1.

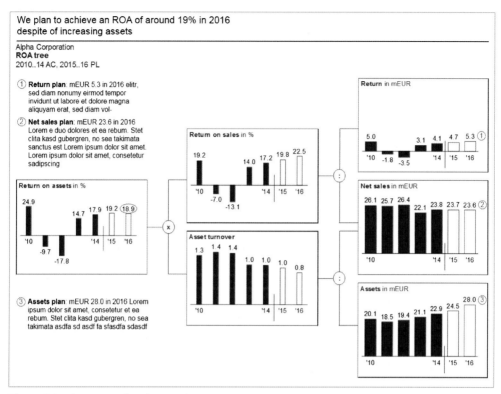

Figure CO 5.2-1: Page showing a ratio tree (example)

CO 5.3 SHOW CHART-TABLE COMBINATIONS

Combining charts and tables on a page is not to be confused with the integration of chart elements in tables.

Chart-table combinations cover situations where a separate chart is added to a page with a table or vice versa. In general, such a combination is very useful if both objects display supplementary data. Tables simply listing the numbers of a chart are superfluous in most cases (see also the UNIFY rule UN 2.3 "Unify the position of legends and labels").

CO 5.4 SHOW CHARTS AND TABLES IN TEXT PAGES

Embedding illuminating charts and tables in the text of a written report helps the reader understanding the message.

Always position charts and tables in close proximity to the phrase carrying the message, which the chart or table supports.

Text pages should contain a title element like other pages. Also use a title - and, if possible, a message - for every chart and table embedded in a text page.

CHECK – ENSURE VISUAL INTEGRITY

CHECK covers all aspects of ensuring visual integrity in reports, presentations and dashboards.

Ensuring visual integrity means that reports present information in the most truthful and the most easily understood way by avoiding misleading visuals.

This chapter covers avoiding manipulated axes and visualization elements, using the same scales, and showing data adjustments.

CH 1 AVOID MANIPULATED AXES

Charts serve as a means to visually compare numerical values. Manipulated axes defeat this purpose of explaining actual interrelations.

CH 1.1 AVOID TRUNCATED AXES

Charts with value axes not starting at zero ("cut" axes) are not "wrong" in and of themselves, but the message to be visually conveyed then does not correspond to the numerical values upon which the chart is based. Therefore, value axes should generally start at zero, see Figure CH 1.1.

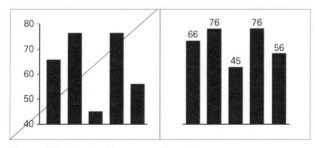

Figure CH 1.1: Avoid truncated axes

One exception to this rule exists: charts with indexed data (e.g. if the value for the index period is set to 100%) with only small variances from 100%. Here "zooming in" on the variances could be of greater value than indicating the absolute values (starting at zero). In this case, position the category labels at the 100% line in order to avoid misinterpretations.

CH 1.2 AVOID LOGARITHMIC AXES

Avoid *logarithmic scales* because they do not allow the visual comparison of values, see Figure CH 1.2. In business, very few applications for logarithmic axes exist (e.g. comparing growth rates of different stocks in percent).

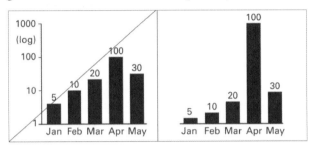

Figure CH 1.2: Avoid logarithmic axes

CH 1.3 AVOID DIFFERENT CLASS SIZES

If the categories represent ordered classes of elements (e.g. age classes) as used for the visualization of distributions in histograms, use class sizes of identical width (e.g. ten years). Otherwise, true visual comparability is impossible, see Figure CH 1.3.

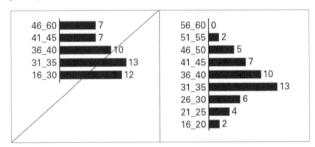

Figure CH 1.3: Avoid different class sizes

CH 2 AVOID MANIPULATED VISUALIZATION ELEMENTS

Displaying values differing by orders of magnitude can be challenging. Use creative solutions instead of clipping visualization elements or cutting value axes.

CH 2.1 AVOID CLIPPED VISUALIZATION ELEMENTS

Similar to "cut" axes, clipped visualization elements such as broken columns make visual comparisons impossible, see Figure CH 2.1.

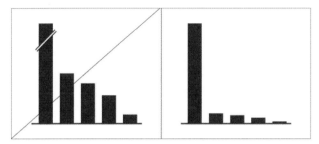

Figure CH 2.1: Avoid clipped visualization elements

CH 2.2 USE CREATIVE SOLUTIONS FOR CHALLENGING SCALING ISSUES

Creative visualization elements can be used to compare extreme values, e.g., displaying data in two-dimensional or even three-dimensional visualization elements allows the comparison of values differing by orders of magnitude, see Figure CH 2.2.

This rule must be clearly separated from the rules of section CH 3 "Avoid misleading representations" where area and volume visualizations are used improperly.

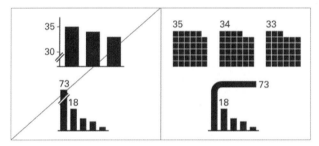

Figure CH 2.2: Use creative solutions for challenging scaling issues

CH 3 AVOID MISLEADING REPRESENTATIONS

Graphical representations are misleading if the visual impression for the observer differs from the underlying values.

CH 3.1 USE CORRECT AREA COMPARISONS, PREFER LINEAR ONES

Using two-dimensional representations (areas of circles, icons, or emblems) for the visualization of data is only valid, if the size of these areas corresponds to the underlying values. The visual perception will be misleading if the values are instead represented by the diameters of circles or the heights of icons. Avoid misunderstanding by using linear comparisons such as columns and bars, see Figure CH 3.1.

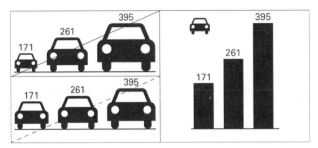

Figure CH 3.1: Use correct area comparisons, prefer linear ones

CH 3.2 USE CORRECT VOLUME COMPARISONS, PREFER LINEAR ONES

Similar to areas, the visual perception will be misleading, if the values are instead represented by the (one-dimensional) diameters or the (two-dimensional) areas of three-dimensional visualization elements (spheres, cubes, etc.). Even if their volumes represent the values, it is hard to perceive them properly. Prefer linear comparisons instead.

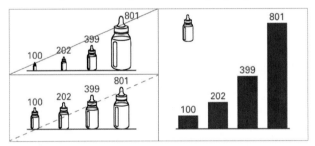

Figure CH 3.2: Use correct volume comparisons, prefer linear ones

CH 3.3 AVOID MISLEADING COLORED AREAS IN MAPS

Different colored areas can be helpful to visualize the precipitation per square meter or the population density. However, do not use colored areas for the visualization of non-area-related figures such as market shares or return on sales. Position columns or bars of identical scale in maps instead. By the way, pie charts also work well here (an exception to the EXPRESS rule EX 2.1 "Replace pie…") because they can be placed precisely at one point, like a city (see Figure CH 3.3).

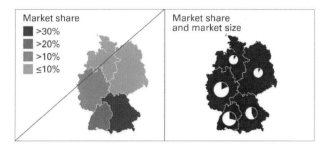

Figure CH 3.3: Avoid misleading colored areas in maps

CH 4   USE THE SAME SCALES

Proper visual comparison requires the usage of identical scales for identical measure units, or – if this is not possible – a clear indication of the difference. If possible, use a consistent scaling concept for the complete report or presentation material.

CH 4.1   USE IDENTICAL SCALE FOR THE SAME UNIT

If presenting more than one chart of the same unit on one page, use the identical scale for these charts, see Figure CH 4.1. In extreme situations identical scales might not be desirable. In these exceptional cases the use of scaling indicators (see CH 4.3 and UN 5.2) can be helpful.

Figure CH 4.1: Use identical scale for the same unit

CH 4.2   SIZE CHARTS TO GIVEN DATA

Using identical scales in multiple charts can be demanding if the values in the charts differ by orders of magnitude. A good solution is adapting the chart size to the given data, see Figure CH 4.2.

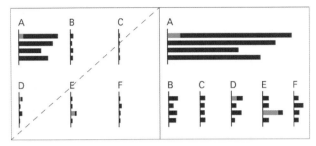

Figure CH 4.2: Size charts to given data

CH 4.3 USE SCALING INDICATORS IF NECESSARY

There are several ways to overcome challenging scaling problems. *Scaling indicators,* such as *scale bands* indicating the same numerical height (typically a power of 10) in all charts are helpful to assist in comparing multiple charts (of the same unit) with different scales, see Figure CH 4.3.

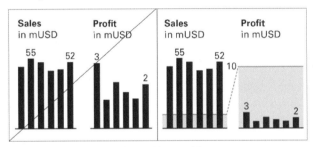

Figure CH 4.3: Use scaling indicators if necessary

IBCS suggest a *semantic design* for scale bands, see SUCCESS rule UN 5.2 "Unify scaling indicators".

CH 4.4 USE OUTLIER INDICATORS IF NECESSARY

Certain values that are very big in comparison to other values are called outliers. If an outlier is not important for business, e.g. a big relative variance of a small value, then it is not appropriate to scale the whole chart to this outlier. Therefore, use *outlier indicators* for unimportant outliers, see Figure CH 4.4.

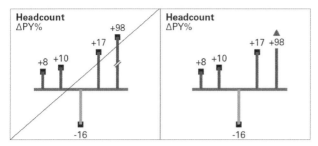

Figure CH 4.4: Use outlier indicators if necessary

IBCS suggest a *semantic design* for outlier indicators, see SUCCESS rule UN 5.3 "Unify outlier indicators".

CH 4.5 USE MAGNIFYING GLASSES

Another way to assist in scaling problems is to use "*magnifying glasses*" for zooming in on a part of a chart with a bigger scale. Use an appropriate visualization element to mark the part of a chart to be zoomed in and to link it to a second chart displaying the zoomed part on a bigger scale.

CH 5 SHOW DATA ADJUSTMENTS

For longer time series, currency and inflationary effects can bias the visual impression, hiding the real development of business.

CH 5.1 SHOW THE IMPACT OF INFLATION

Making inflation effects transparent helps avoid misinterpretations of time series visualizations, see Figure CH 5.1.

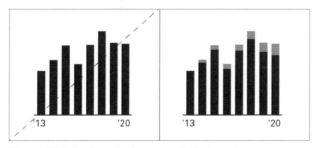

Figure CH 5.1: Show the impact of inflation

CH 5.2 SHOW THE CURRENCY IMPACT

Similar to inflation effects, the adjustment of currency effects can help to avoid misinterpretations, see Figure CH 5.2.

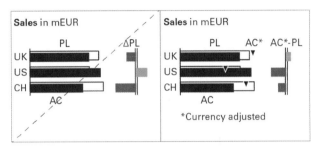

Figure CH 5.2: Show the currency impact

TABLE OF FIGURES

TERMS AND REFERENCES

Y

year-to-date analysis *33*
YTD *33*

YTG *34*

Z

Zelazny, Gene *iv, 67*

After studying the IBCS standards, you may be looking for additional resources to deepen your understanding.

IBCS WITH SUCCESS POSTER
98 RULES IN PICTURES

This poster reminds you every day how to make your reports, presentations and dashboards more understandable. 98 pictures covering the SUCCESS formula, corresponding exactly with the contents of the IBCS Standards.

You have two options:

Get a hardcopy of the poster (Europe and North America only).

Get the PDF of the poster and print it yourself.

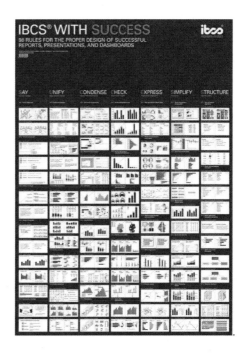

NOTATION MANUAL
TEMPLATE FOR A COMPANY SPECIFIC REPORT NOTATION MANUAL

Want to enforce adoption of a consistent report notation by creating your own manual for the design of IBCS compliant reports, presentations, and dashboards?

There is an IBCS template for creating company specific notation manuals. 50 pages in 16:9 format illustrated with numerous instructive figures. Either in PDF format or as a fully editable PPT template.

Get the notation manual template on ibcs-shop.com.

SOLID, OUTLINED, HATCHED
HOW VISUAL CONSISTENCY HELPS BETTER UNDERSTAND REPORTS, PRESENTATIONS AND DASHBOARDS

Get the book by Rolf Hichert and Jürgen Faisst

Read the story behind the semantic notation of IBCS. The authors transfer the principle of "notation standards" commonly found in many disciplines such as music or engineering to business communication. They develop a visual reporting language and apply it to the charts and tables used in business reports, presentation slides and interactive dashboards. Practical examples prove: They are on the right track.

Get the book on Amazon.

Watch the corresponding video course

35 digestible lessons of 5 to 10 minutes. Most of them are videos enriched with polls, quizzes and exercises. You also get a workbook which you can fill to perform the exercises. After finishing a section you can check your learning progress with the help of a test.

Enroll on ibcs.teachable.com.

IBCS® CERTIFIED ANALYST TRAINING
UNDERSTAND AND APPLY IBCS

Understand the SUCCESS formula of IBCS and learn how to apply it in practice. This course is offered inhouse or in open courses both online and classroom. Followed by an online test for becoming an IBCS® Certified Analyst.

Find this and more training courses on ibcs.com/training.

Made in the USA
Las Vegas, NV
15 March 2022

45669839R00102